contents

WHERE TO STAY AND WHAT TO DO IN

Baker

London Tourist Board and Convention Bureau, Glen House, Stag Place, London SW1E 5LT
Tel: (020) 7932 2000 **Fax:** (020) 7932 0222
Editor: Jenny Kite **Managing Editor:** Diana James.

London Tourist Board and Convention Bureau (LTB) is the official tourist organisation for Greater London, financed by membership subscriptions and certain commercial activities. In addition LTB receives financial support from the Department for Culture, Media and Sport, the English Tourism Council and the London Boroughs Grants Scheme.

Published for London Tourist Board and Convention Bureau by: Book Production Consultants PLC, 25-27 High Street, Chesterton, Cambridge CB4 1ND
Tel: (01223) 352790 **Fax:** (01223) 460718
E-mail: ltbpubs@bpccam.co.uk
URL: www.bpccam.co.uk
Advertisement Sales: Mongoose Communications Ltd, Victory House, Leicester Square, London WC2H 7QH
Tel: (020) 7306 0300 **Fax:** (020) 7306 0301.
Design by: Miller Design Partnership, London
Printed in Great Britain by: The Burlington Press, Cambridge. Distributed by the publications division of the Automobile Association, Fanum House, Basingstoke, Hants RG21 2EA. The information contained in this guide was supplied by the proprietors in the summer of 2000 and while every effort has been made to ensure accuracy in describing the facilities offered, London Tourist Board and Convention Bureau and Book Production Consultants cannot be held responsible for any errors or omissions. No part may be reproduced without written permission from the publisher.
© London Tourist Board 2000 **ISBN:** 0 946837 66 X

Please mention '**where to stay and what to do in London**' when contacting organisations featured in this publication.

For a free copy of '**London capital breaks**', London Tourist Board's free guide to London, giving details of opening hours, admission prices of many attractions and much more, write to **London Tourist Board** at the address above.

HOTELS AND BED AND BREAKFASTS

Over the last two years an amazing array of new museums, galleries and attractions have opened in London, making it, more than ever, the place to visit.

something for everyone
in 21st-century London

THE LATEST AND GREATEST

No trip to London would be complete without a trip on the **British Airways London Eye**. See the city and its landmarks from a completely new angle – 135 metres above terra firma!

Don't miss the new **Tate Modern** on London's South Bank. This converted power station houses one of the greatest collections of contemporary art in the world but it's worth visiting for the building alone. Tate Modern also has a café, restaurant and fantastic shop, so make sure you put a few hours aside. Entry to the gallery is free.

Somerset House on Embankment is now fully accessible to the public for the first time in its long history. Once the site of several government departments, Somerset House is home to the Courtauld Gallery of impressionist art and the Gilbert Collection of decorative arts. Somerset House has a stunning courtyard that hosts events and performances in the summer months, and there is also a great terrace and café where you can watch the world go by.

The British Museum Great Court will open to the public in late 2000. This £97 million redevelopment features a giant steel and glass roof over the courtyard. The museum offers free entry and a wealth of ancient artefacts and galleries to explore.

The Wellcome Wing is the latest addition to the Science Museum. A 'breathtaking theatre of contemporary science', it includes interactive exhibitions and a 3D IMAX cinema.

England's oldest public art gallery, Dulwich Picture Gallery, displays a magnificent collection of 17th- and 18th-century European Old Master paintings. Its recent refurbishment has increased gallery space and created a new café.

For a different kind of attraction altogether, visit the Wetland Centre, Barnes, in London's south west. This new home for London's wetland flora and fauna was created from more than 100 acres of disused reservoir. There is a state-of-the-art visitor centre, café and plenty of viewing hides.

ON THE HISTORY TRAIL

The great thing about London is that all these new and redeveloped attractions stand alongside some of the most historic buildings in the world.

One of the most visited attractions in London is the Tower of London, home of intrigue and gruesome deeds for almost 1,000 years. It's much tamer now, but costumed guides and Yeoman Warders can recount tales from the Tower's colourful history for its visitors. The Tower is also home to the Crown Jewels and the famous ravens.

Syon House in Brentford is the London home of the Duke of Northumberland. Set in 200 acres of parkland and gardens, designed by Capability Brown, the turbulent history of Syon House stretches back more than 400 years.

The magnificent Hampton Court Palace was a favourite residence of Henry VIII. Here you can enjoy more than 500 years of royal history and see the Tudor kitchens, tennis court and state apartments. Enjoy the extensive gardens on the banks of the River Thames.

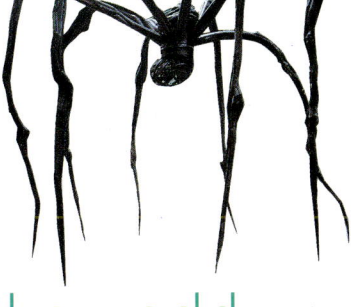

...one of the greatest collections of contemporary art in the world

Eltham Palace in the city's south east is an extraordinary blend of architecture. Here you can see the banqueting hall of the medieval palace attached to a fabulous Art Deco home. Eltham Palace sits in extensive, beautiful gardens — a perfect place for a picnic.

It's a modern replica, but Shakespeare's Globe looks every bit the real thing. This is a fitting tribute to one of the world's greatest playwrights and to Elizabethan theatre. A definite 'must see' for Shakespeare fans.

Nearby, Southwark Cathedral is London's oldest Gothic church (c.1220). It houses a number of interesting memorials to Shakespeare and the Elizabethan theatres of Bankside.

If you want a good overview of London's history, visit the Museum of London Here you'll find the tale of the city from pre-Roman times to the present day. Highlights include 'The Great Fire Experience' and reconstructed Victorian shops.

LONDON FOR FREE

Some of London's most loved visitor attractions offer free admission (except for special events and exhibitions).

The National Gallery in Trafalgar Square displays an extensive range of Western European painting from the 13th century to the 1900s. Some of the famous artists on show include Botticelli, Leonardo da Vinci, Turner, Renoir and Cézanne.

Just around the corner is the National Portrait Gallery, which has a permanent collection of portraits from the Middle Ages to the present day. There is a new gallery housing Tudor portraits and a roof top restaurant with spectacular views.

The Geffrye Museum in East London displays period rooms, furniture and decorative arts from 1600 to the present day. Kenwood House is a neo-classical mansion set in the leafy surrounds of Hampstead. It has stunning interiors and a renowned art collection featuring works by Turner, Rembrandt and Reynolds.

Tate Britain at Millbank holds the national collection of British painting from 1500 to the present day, including works by Blake, Constable, Gainsborough, Hirst, Hockney and Turner. There is a full programme of special exhibitions throughout the year.

GREAT FOR FAMILIES

Many of London's leading museums and galleries, including the Natural History Museum and the National Maritime Museum, offer free admission for kids and senior citizens, while others offer family discounts. Make the most of these incentives to enjoy London's finest attractions with the family.

The Natural History Museum in South Kensington is a fantastic gothic building with lots of creepy crawlies and dinosaur bones to captivate kids.

Another place for creatures of all kinds is London Zoo, where you can see the Web of Life. This biodiversity exhibition is a great place for kids to learn about conservation and get close to animals from ants to anteaters.

A similar experience can be had at the London Aquarium, home to hundreds of species of fish and marine life. There is a shark tank and 'beach' area for touching friendly rays.

The National Maritime Museum in Greenwich offers a comprehensive tour of Britain's maritime history, with life-size and model ships, paintings and navigation equipment. There are lots of interactive displays to keep children entertained.

...enjoy London's finest attractions with the family

Kids of any age will enjoy the Bethnal Green Museum of Childhood, with its superb collection of toys, dolls, dolls' houses, puppets, toy theatres and games, children's costume and nursery furniture.

opposite page top left Trafalgar Square **top right** Tate Britain **bottom left** Shakespeare's Globe Theatre **bottom right** Elephant weighing © London Zoo **this page top** Natural History Museum © Jean Miller **bottom left** The Queen's House, Greenwich © National Maritime Museum **right** London Aquarium

MUSIC, DANCE, FILM AND MORE...

Lovers of opera and ballet should visit the redeveloped **Royal Opera House** in Covent Garden. As well as performances in the stunning main theatre, visitors can enjoy free lunch-time concerts and backstage tours.

Sadler's Wells has also benefited from recent redevelopment. This state-of-the-art venue offers the very latest in ballet and dance.

Other major arts venues around the city include the **Barbican Centre** and the **South Bank Centre**, both offering a comprehensive programme of concerts, film, theatre and exhibitions.

London has more than 125 cinemas offering the latest releases as well as old favourites.

EAT AROUND THE WORLD IN LONDON

Indian, Italian, African, modern British, Thai, French, Moroccan... the choice of cuisine available in London goes on and on (and on) and it's available in more than 6,000 restaurants and 3,000 cafes and bars across the city.

You might like to try your own gourmet safari of international destinations while you're staying in London. These are just a few suggestions:

Soho Spice and **Red Fort**, both in Soho, offer excellent Indian cuisine. There is also an excellent range of Bengali restaurants in Brick Lane.

For high quality Italian cuisine in elegant surroundings try Sir Terence Conran's **Sartoria** on Savile Row.

Chez Gerard offers fantastic French food in six restaurants in central London locations. It's renowned for the 'best steak frites this side of Paris'. **Brasserie St Quentin** in Knightsbridge offers classic Parisian cuisine in equally classic surroundings.

Far East cuisine can be found at **Jim Thompson's Oriental Bar, Restaurant and Bazaar** on King's Road and restaurants in **Chinatown**, Soho. There are too many different types of cuisine in London to mention here but you can visit **EatLondon.net** for a more comprehensive listing.

opposite page top
Her Majesty's Theatre, Haymarket
bottom The Royal Ballet © David Bailey
this page top Theatre Museum
bottom left Nobu Restaurant, Metropolitan Hotel **right** Brick Lane

OPEN TO NON-RESIDENTS

Some of London's best restaurants can be found in hotels and you don't have to be staying there to enjoy them.

Axis at **Number One Aldwych** serves Modern British food in the heart of the West End.

For one of the best views, as well as the best food, visit **Windows** at the **London Hilton** on Park Lane.

I-Thai at **The Hempel** offers exotic and intriguing cuisine, a mix of Thai, Italian and Japanese.

Elegant French cuisine can be found at Marco Pierre White's **The Oak Room** at **Le Méridien** Piccadilly.

PUB CULTURE

Britain is world renowned for its pubs and there are 3,000 to choose from in London. Some of the finest are situated along the River Thames, including the beautifully restored **Trafalgar Tavern** in Greenwich, and the **Blue Anchor** in Hammersmith. Most pubs also serve food, ranging from simple, hearty meals to the very latest in international and modern British cuisine.

top Ruperts, Old Compton Street
bottom left Trafalgar Tavern, Greenwich
right Limelight

INTO THE EARLY HOURS

London has a huge clubbing and late night bar scene so there's no reason to go home early if you don't want to.

Zeta at the **London Hilton** offers 'healthy' cocktails and delicious food in relaxed and stylish surroundings.

Motcombs Club in Knightsbridge has a DJ and open bar until 0300; guests can also eat in the restaurant until 0130.

Limelight is a renowned London nightclub set in a converted chapel with two floors of music.

A great range of gay pubs and clubs can be found in Old Compton Street, Soho.

For clubbing information pick up the weekly listings guide *Time Out*.

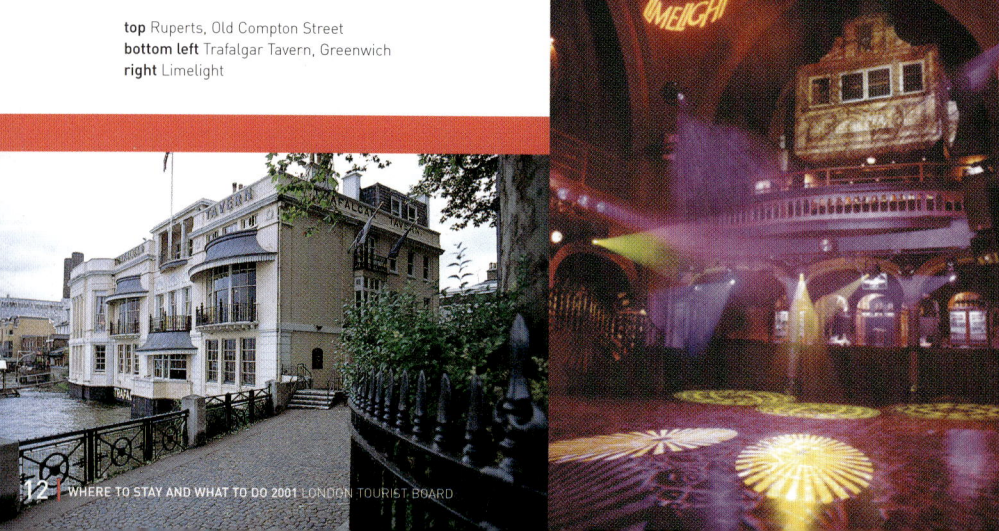

WHILE IN LONDON SEE OUR FAMOUS BEAUTY SPOTS.

London's winners

Winners and Highly Commended entries for the London Tourism Awards 2000

LARGE ATTRACTION
TOWER OF LONDON

The **Tower of London** encapsulates 1,000 years of London's history. Visitors can see the unique Crown Jewels and experience the excitement of being inside a working palace with its troops. Tours are also available with the Yeoman Warders, whose knowledge of and enthusiasm for the Tower are unsurpassed. Recent innovations for this world class site include the Domesday Book display and Thomas More's cell.
Tel: (020) 7709 0765 **Highly commended:** The Museum of London/The Science Museum

SMALL ATTRACTION
ELTHAM PALACE

With its stunning mix of medieval and Art Deco architecture, its extensive gardens and its wealth of history, **Eltham Palace** is an attraction with something for everyone. English Heritage undertook to refurbish the property in 1998 – recreating rooms and installing facilities to make the house and gardens accessible to wheelchair users. The quality of information and interpretation on offer is first class.
Tel: (020) 8294 2548
Highly commended: The Jewish Museum

HOTEL OF THE YEAR (OVER 50 BEDROOMS)
FOUR SEASONS HOTEL LONDON

For a taste of pure luxury, stay in the **Four Seasons Hotel London** on Park Lane. The customer care and facilities are impeccable and the surroundings are stylish and relaxing. The hotel has a very welcoming atmosphere and the best in customer service is offered. There are also good facilities for disabled guests.
Tel: (020) 7499 0888

HOTEL OF THE YEAR (UNDER 50 BEDROOMS)
THE COLONNADE

This stunning townhouse offers luxurious, homely accommodation with attentive service. The furnishings, bathrooms and public areas are of a very high quality and the young, enthusiastic staff work hard to make sure each guest has a memorable stay.
Tel: (020) 7286 1052

BED AND BREAKFAST ACCOMMODATION
NUMBER SIXTEEN

Number Sixteen is a townhouse style bed and breakfast with high quality accommodation and décor and attentive staff. **Number Sixteen** tries to create a 'home away from home' for guests with a welcoming atmosphere and comfortable rooms. The recent refurbishment has further improved the appeal of the property.
Tel: (020) 7589 5232

INNOVATION IN TOURISM
HEATHROW EXPRESS

The **Heathrow Express** check-in facility at Paddington offers a convenient, quick journey between central London and the airport. The automatic ticket machine offering multi-lingual instructions and the ability to pay in eight currencies is particularly useful for the visitor.
Tel: (020) 0845 600 1515

TOURISM FOR ALL
BBC EXPERIENCE AND NATIONAL MARITIME MUSEUM

The **BBC Experience** has created facilities for wheelchair users, the blind/partially sighted and hearing-impaired guests, as well as those with special educational needs. They have also added subtitles to many of the TV clips on show and signed others.

The **National Maritime Museum** has superb new spaces and exhibitions, all of which are wheelchair accessible. In addition to providing braille and large print guides, the Museum has sign-interpreted programmes and, a pioneering deaf astronomers' club, and is currently working on astronomy shows for the visually impaired.
BBC Experience tel: (020) 0870 603 0304,
National Maritime Museum tel: (020) 8858 4422

SUSTAINABLE TOURISM
THE NATIONAL MARITIME MUSEUM

The **National Maritime Museum** has a strong commitment to the local community and encourages its staff to become involved in environmental initiatives. The museum played a significant role in gaining World Heritage Site status for Maritime Greenwich and is represented on a number of organisations safeguarding the development of Greenwich. The museum actively encourages its visitors to use public transport
Tel: (020) 8858 4422
Highly commended: London Zoo

LONDON WORLD CLASS WELCOME
MICHAEL BENSON, ADDINGTON PALACE

Michael Benson has been the curator and on-site historian at **Addington Palace**, the former retreat of the Archbishops of Canterbury, for almost thirty years. He has been chosen for the London World Class Welcome award for his attention to detail and his desire to make each tour of the house unique. He epitomises the enthusiasm, pride and commitment which ambassadors for London need to have.
Tel: (020) 8862 5000 **Highly commended:** James Doyle, Crowne-Plaza London Heathrow

TOURIST INFORMATION CENTRE
GREENWICH

Greenwich Tourist Information Centre has a wide range of information in a variety of formats, including public access kiosks for information on Greenwich's facilities at the touch of a button. The staff are very helpful and can provide comprehensive information on all the attractions in the area and make accommodation bookings on your behalf.
Tel: (020) 8858 6376
Highly commended: Swanley

SIGHTSEEING TOUR OF THE YEAR
THE BIG BUS COMPANY

The Big Bus Company has an excellent commentary with innovative tips on London for the visitor. Advice covers where to go for afternoon tea, the quirks of English pub opening hours and the workings of local taxis. You can choose between tours with recorded or live commentary, both of which are very animated, informative and enthusiastic.
Tel: (020) 7233 9533

SEE WHERE HENRY VIII'S WIVES LOST THEIR *heads.*

‡ Visitor Attraction of the Year 2000, London Tourist Board Awards.

‡ Stand on the execution site of three British queens and see the historic 'Instruments of Torture'.

‡ Hear the myths and legends when you go on a free Yeoman Warder 'Beefeater' tour.

‡ Marvel at the CROWN JEWELS and experience 900 years of royal history.

‡ Don't miss Thomas More's cell and Domesday Book, on display this year only. And try your luck in the Great Crown Jewels Robbery this half-term, from October 21st-29th.

‡ Nearest tube - Tower Hill.

THE TOWER *of* LONDON
The Royal Fortress on the Thames
www.hrp.org.uk

tourist information services

Visitorcall is the London Tourist Board's comprehensive range of recorded information services. It is available 24 hours a day and updated daily. Visitorcall has been created so that you can quickly and easily select the answer to your question or, if you prefer, listen to up-to-date listings of current and forthcoming events. See page 30 for a full listing.

Accommodation reservations can be made throughout London. Call the London Tourist Board's Telephone Accommodation Booking Service on (020) 7932 2020 with your requirements and Mastercard/Visa/Switch details. Service available from January 2001.

* Accommodation reservations

POINT OF ARRIVAL

* **Heathrow Terminals 1,2,3 Underground Station Concourse**, Heathrow Airport, TW6 2JA.
Open: Daily 0800-1800; 1 Jun-30 Sep, Mon-Sat 0800-1900, Sun 0800-1800.

* **Liverpool Street Underground Station**, EC2M 7PN.
Open: Daily 0800-1800; 1 Jun-30 Sep, Mon-Sat 0800-1900, Sun 0800-1800.

* **Victoria Station Forecourt**, SW1V 1JU.
Open: 1 Jun-30 Sep, Mon-Sat 0800-2100, Sun 0800-1800; 1 Oct-Easter, daily 0800-1800; Easter-31 May, Mon-Sat 0800-2000, Sun 0800-1800.

* **Waterloo International Terminal**, Arrivals Hall, London SE1 7LT.
Open: Daily 0830-2230.

INNER LONDON

* **Britain Visitor Centre**, 1 Regent Street, Piccadilly Circus, SW1Y 4XT.
Open: Mon 0930-1830, Tue-Fri 0900-1830, Sat & Sun 1000-1600; Jun-Oct, Sat 0900-1700.

* **Greenwich TIC**, Pepys House, 2 Cutty Sark Gardens, Greenwich SE10 9LW.
Tel: 0870 608 2000; Fax: (020) 8853 4607.
Open: Daily 1000-1700; 1 Jul-31 Aug, daily 1000-2000.

Lewisham TIC, Lewisham Library, 199-201 Lewisham High Street, SE13 6LG. Tel: (020) 8297 8317.
Open: Mon 1000-1700, Tue-Fri 0900-1700, Sat 1000-1600.

* **Southwark Information Centre**, London Bridge, 6 Tooley Street, SE1 2SY. Tel: (020) 7403 8299.

Open: Easter-31 Oct, Mon-Sat 1000-1800, Sun 1030-1730; 1 Nov-Easter, Mon-Sat 1000-1600, Sun 1100-1600

Tower Hamlets TIC, 18 Lamb Street, E1 6EA.
Fax: (020) 7375 2539.
Open: Mon, Tue, Thu & Fri 0930-1330 & 1430-1630, Wed 0930-1300, Sun 1130-1430.

OUTER LONDON

Bexley Hall Place Visitor Centre, Bourne Road, Bexley, Kent DA5 1PQ.
Tel: (01322) 558676; Fax: (01322) 522921.
Open: Mon-Sat 1000-1630, Sun 1400-1730.

* **Croydon TIC**, Katharine Street, Croydon CR9 1ET.
Tel: (020) 8253 1009; Fax: (020) 8253 1008.
Open: Mon-Wed 0900-1800, Thu 0930-1800, Fri 0900-1800, Sat 0900-1700, Sun 1400-1700.

Harrow TIC, Civic Centre, Station Road, Harrow HA1 2XF.
Tel: (020) 8424 1103; Fax: (020) 8424 1134.
Open: Mon-Fri 0900-1700.

Hillingdon TIC, Central Library, 14 High Street, Uxbridge UB8 1HD.
Tel: (01895) 250706; Fax: (01895) 239794.
Open: Mon, Tue & Thu 0930-2000, Wed 0930-1730, Fri 1000-1730, Sat 0930-1600.

* **Hounslow TIC**, 24 The Treaty Centre, Hounslow High Street, Hounslow TW3 1ES.
Tel: (020) 8583 2929; Fax: (020) 8583 4714.
Open: Mon, Wed, Fri & Sat 0930-1730, Tue & Thu 0930-2000.

Kingston TIC, Market House, Market Place, Kingston upon Thames KT1 1JS.
Tel: (020) 8547 5592; Fax: (020) 8547 5594.
Open: Mon-Fri 1000-1700, Sat 0900-1600.

* **Richmond TIC**, Old Town Hall, Whittaker Avenue, Richmond TW9 1TP.
Tel: (020) 8940 9125; Fax: (020) 8940 6899.
Open: Mon-Sat 1000-1700, Easter Sunday-end Sep, Sun 1030-1330.

* **Swanley TIC**, London Road, Kent BR8 7AE.
Tel: (01322) 614660.
Open: Mon-Thu 0930-1730, Fri 0930-1800, Sat 0900-1600.

Twickenham TIC, The Atrium, Civic Centre, York Street, Twickenham, Middlesex TW1 3BZ.
Tel: (020) 8891 7272.
Open: Mon-Thu 0900-1715, Fri 0900-1700.

travel information

TRAVELLING BETWEEN LONDON AND ITS AIRPORTS

Gatwick Tel. (01293) 535353
⇄ The Gatwick Express leaves every 15 minutes to Victoria Station, every 30 minutes at night. The journey takes about 30 minutes. There is also the Thameslink service to the City and King's Cross. Tel. 08457 484950.

Gatwick Airport Station is in the South Terminal, and linked to other parts by escalators and lifts. A Transit Shuttle runs continuously between the South and North Terminals.

Airbus Airbus A5 goes to Victoria Coach Station, with stops at Chessington (outside World of Adventures) and Wandsworth (Armoury Way, Stop D). Tel. 0870 574 7777.

Coach National Express. Tel. 0990 808080. The services operate to Victoria Coach Station, where there are connections to all parts of Britain. Journey time is about 55 minutes.

Heathrow Tel. 0870 000 0123
⊖ The Piccadilly line connects the airport to Central London and the rest of the underground system. The trains have special luggage areas. The journey to Piccadilly Circus takes about 47 minutes. There are trains every few minutes. There are two stations in the airport: Heathrow Terminals 1, 2, 3, and Heathrow Terminal 4. Check which terminal applies to your flight. Tel. (020) 7222 1234.

⇄ The Heathrow Express runs from Paddington Station to Heathrow Airport (stops for Terminals, 1, 2, 3 and for Terminal 4) every 15 minutes from 0510-2340. Journey time is 15-20 minutes. Tel. 0845 600 1515.

Airbus Airbus A2 goes to King's Cross, with stops at Notting Hill Gate, Bayswater Road, Marble Arch, Marylebone Road, Euston and Russell Square. Tel. 0870 574 7777.

London City Tel. (020) 7646 0000
A shuttle bus departs from Liverpool Street Station (journey time 25 minutes), Canary Wharf Station (journey time 10 minutes) and from Canning Town Station (journey time 5-7 minutes).

Luton Tel. (01582) 405100
⇄ There is a combined rail and coach link from King's Cross Thameslink to the airport, via Luton Station. Journey time is about 45-60 minutes.

Coach Green Line 757 operates from Buckingham Palace Road, Victoria, to the airport, taking about 75-90 minutes. Tel. 0870 608 7261.

Stansted Tel. (01279) 680500
⇄ A direct service from Liverpool Street takes about 45 minutes. The train stops at Tottenham Hale, giving direct access to the Victoria line of the underground. Tel. 08457 484950.

Airbus Airbus goes to Victoria rail and coach stations; A7 via Stratford and A6 via Hendon, both with several stops en route. Tel. 0870 574 7777.

Coach National Express operates from Victoria Coach Station, taking about 80 minutes. Tel. 0990 808080.

TRAVELLING IN AND FROM LONDON

Bus and Underground
For information about bus or underground services in Greater London, or the Docklands Light Railway, telephone (020) 7222 1234 at any time.

There are enquiry offices for personal callers at: each of the arrivals halls at Heathrow Airport; Victoria, Euston, Paddington and Liverpool Street Rail Stations; West Croydon, Brent Cross and Hammersmith Bus Stations; underground stations: King's Cross, North Greenwich, Oxford Circus, Piccadilly Circus, Heathrow Terminals 1, 2, 3, Heathrow Terminal 4 and St James's Park.

Visitors should take advantage of inclusive tickets such as the daily or weekly Travelcards, available from stations or information offices.

Car
Numerous international and British car hire

companies have offices at the airports and in London. Charges may be calculated by the duration of hire, by the mileage, or both.

Motoring clubs offer emergency services. For the Automobile Association, Tel. 0800 887766; for the Royal Automobile Club, Tel. 0800 828282.

On-street parking in Central London is expensive and difficult. Illegal parking is controlled by fines, towing away of vehicles, and wheel clamps. Restrictions are shown by yellow lines on the road and kerb, and yellow plates on lamp posts. Parking is particularly restricted between 0830 and 1830 Monday to Friday, and from 0830 to 1330 on Saturday.
National Car Parks: Tel. (020) 7499 7050.

Coach
National Express operates to all parts of Britain. Most coaches leave from Victoria Coach Station, Tel. 0990 808080.

Green Line operate to many interesting places around London, such as Windsor and Hampton Court. Tel. 0870 608 7261.

Rail
National train enquiries,
Tel. 08457 484950
Continental train enquiries,
Tel. 0870 584 8848

Taxis
Taxis may be hailed in the street; the doorman will do it for you at your hotel. Taxis may be booked by telephoning (020) 7272 0272 or (020) 7253 5000. Extra charges, such as for evening and weekend journeys, are displayed inside the cab.

Drivers are not obliged to accept a hiring of over six miles, or over 20 miles for a journey from London Heathrow Airport, but if they do, and the journey is wholly within the London area, the fare payable is as shown on the meter. If a driver accepts a hiring to a destination outside the Greater London area, the fare becomes negotiable, and should be agreed beforehand.

Do not use unauthorised drivers who offer their services at airports and stations.

ADVICE

Bureaux de Change
Banks are normally open from 0900 to 1630 or later, Monday to Friday. Some branches may open on Saturdays. Bureaux de Change are open longer hours than ordinary banks. Many are near railway stations and in shopping areas. You are advised only to use those displaying the official Tourist Board symbol and code of conduct. Check both rates and commission.

Lost Property
Rail
Enquire at station of arrival.

National Express
Enquire at Victoria Coach Station.

London Transport
Enquire at Lost Property Office,
200 Baker Street, NW1,
open Mon-Fri 0930-1400.
Recorded Tel. (020) 7486 2496
Fax. (020) 7918 1028.

Taxis
Contact: Metropolitan Police Lost Property Office,
15 Penton Street, London N1 9PU,
or Tel. (020) 7833 0996.
Open Mon-Fri 0900-1600.

Theatre and Concert Tickets
Tickets may be bought from the Britain Visitor Centre in Regent Street and the tourist information centres in Victoria and Waterloo stations. They may also be bought direct from the theatre box office, in person or by telephone. Most theatres accept credit card bookings. There are also many theatre booking agents. Always check for the amount of commission or booking fee. Do not buy from touts.

Tipping
Cab drivers expect to be tipped about 10 per cent of the fare. Restaurants sometimes add a service charge of 10-15 per cent. This should be shown on the menu. Tipping of staff such as chambermaids and porters is discretionary but it is usual to tip guides at the end of sightseeing tours.

Sightseeing Tours
One of the best ways to see London is on a guided tour. Tours may be booked at your hotel or at the Britain Visitor Centre in Regent Street and the tourist information centres in Victoria and Waterloo stations. Members of London Tourist Board who operate sightseeing tours use registered 'Blue Badge' guides, who have passed a thorough examination. Such guides wear blue badges. Also popular are walking tours, and river or canal trips. Tourist Information Centres have leaflets with details.

PUBLIC HOLIDAYS IN ENGLAND AND WALES, 2001

New Year's Day	1 January
Good Friday	13 April
Easter Monday	16 April
May Bank Holiday	7 May
Spring Bank Holiday	28 May
Summer Bank Holiday	27 August
Christmas Day	25 December
Boxing Day	26 December

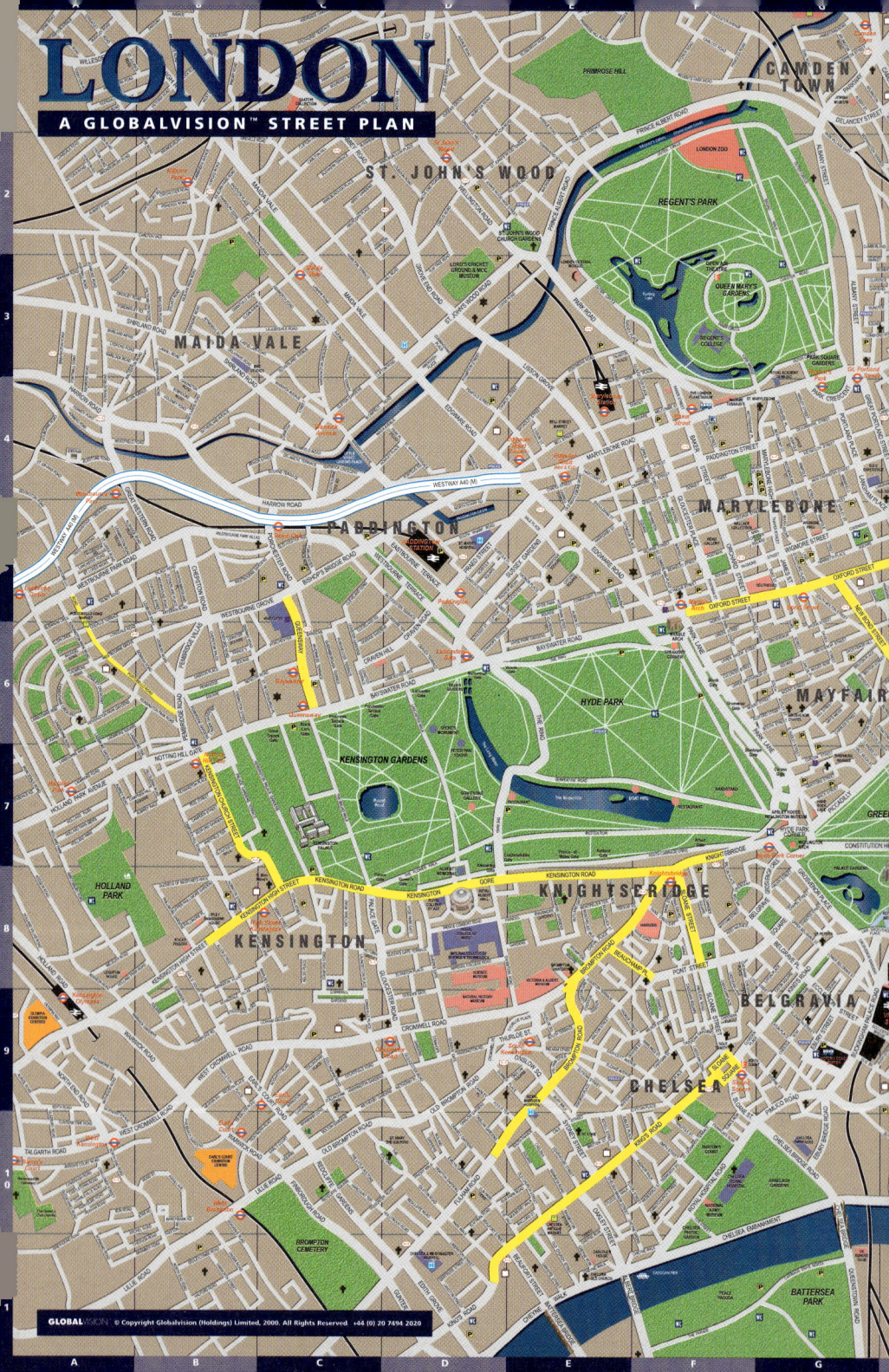

arrival, it may be advisable to see your room first to ensure that it meets your requirements.

CANCELLATIONS

When you accept offered accommodation on the telephone or in writing, you may be entering into a legally binding contract with the proprietor of the establishment. This means that if you cancel a reservation, fail to take up the accommodation or leave prematurely the proprietor may be entitled to compensation if it cannot be re-let for all or a good part of the booked period. If a deposit has been paid it is likely to be forfeited and an additional payment may be demanded.

However, no such claim can be made by the proprietor until after the booked period, during which time every effort should be made to re-let it. Any circumstances which might lead to repudiation of contract may also need to be taken into account and, in the case of a dispute, legal advice should be sought by both parties. It is therefore in your interest to advise the management immediately if you have to change your travel plans, cancel a booking or leave prematurely.

COMMENTS AND COMPLAINTS

Accommodation establishments have a number of legal and statutory responsibilities toward their customers in areas such as giving information on prices, providing adequate fire precautions and safeguarding valuables. Like other businesses, they must also meet the requirements of the Trade Descriptions Acts 1968 and 1972 when describing and offering accommodation and facilities.

The establishment descriptions and other details appearing in this guide have been provided by proprietors themselves who have signed a declaration that the information conforms with the requirements of the Trade Descriptions Acts. The prices given in the listings are estimates, intended as a guide only and can be subject to change. Prices and other details should always be carefully checked at the time of booking.

We hope that you will not have any cause for complaint but problems do inevitably occur from time to time. If you are dissatisfied, make your complaint to the management at the time of the incident. This gives the management an opportunity to take action at once to investigate and to put things right without delay. The longer a complaint is left the more difficult it is to deal with it effectively.

In certain circumstances LTB may look into complaints. However, the Board has no statutory control over registered establishments or their methods of operation and cannot become involved in legal or contractual matters.

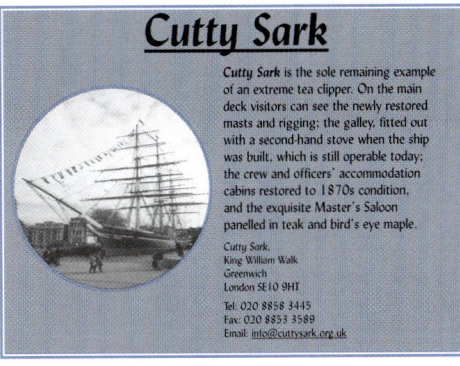
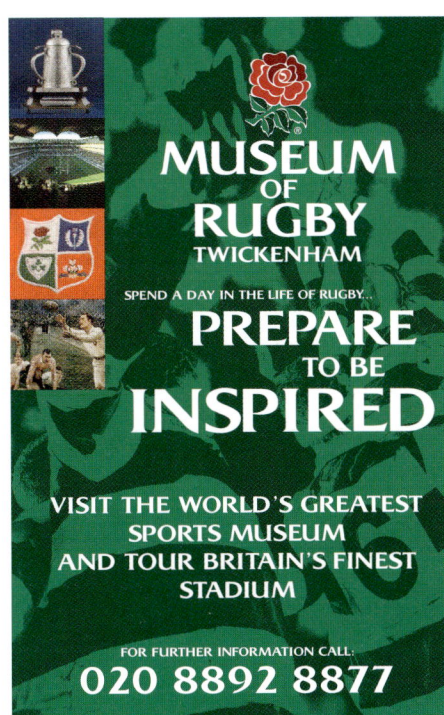

Inner London Area Map

MAIN HOTEL AREAS IN CENTRAL LONDON

SW1 – Victoria/Westminster
W1 – West End/Mayfair/Oxford Street
WC1/WC2 – Bloomsbury/Strand/Leicester Square
W2 – Paddington/Bayswater
SW3/5/7 – Chelsea/Earl's Court/South Kensington

OTHER AREAS IN LONDON

EC1/2/3/4 – City of London
W8/11/14 – Kensington/Notting Hill Gate/Holland Park
W3/4/5/6/7/12 – Acton/Chiswick/Ealing /Hammersmith
North West London
North London
South West London
East London
South East London
London's Country

Good Value Accommodation
in Central London
Central Reservations Telephone (020) 7402 0202

Abbey Court and Westpoint Hotel

- ☑ Pleasant central location
- ☑ Convenient location 2 minutes from Paddington Station & Heathrow Express, & 4 minutes from Airbus
- ☑ Easy access to all London's important tourist sights, shopping districts, theatres, Oxford Street and Piccadilly Circus
- ☑ En-Suite shower & w.c. in all rooms

- ☑ Lift to all floors
- ☑ Each room with colour T.V., radio & telephone
- ☑ Car parking by arrangement

Abbey Court and Westpoint Hotel
170-174 Sussex Gardens
Hyde Park London W2 1TP
Tel (020) 7402 0704
Fax (020) 7262 2055
*www.*westpointhotel.com
e-mail info@westpointhotel.com
Tel (020) 7402 0281
Fax (020) 7224 9114
*www.*abbeycourt.com
e-mail info@abbeycourt.com

RATES	LOW SEASON	HIGH SEASON
Singles	from £48.00	from £56.00
Doubles *pp*	from £32.00	from £37.00
Triples *pp*	from £26.00	from £28.00
Family Room *pp*	from £22.00	from £24.00

Sass House Hotel

Central London hotel located within two minutes walk from Hyde Park. Most rooms with private showers/toilets. All rooms have colour TV and radio. Easy access to all tourist attractions – within 5 minutes walking distance of Lancaster Gate and Paddington underground/ mainline stations and Heathrow Express.

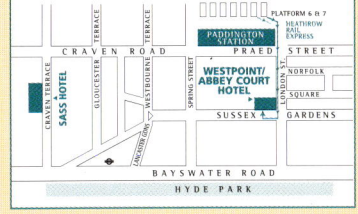

RATES	LOW SEASON	HIGH SEASON
Twin *pp*	from £26.00	from £29.00
Doubles *pp*	from £24.50	from £28.00
Triples *pp*	from £22.00	from £24.00
Family Room *pp*	from £19.50	from £21.50

Sass House Hotel
11 Craven Terrace,
Hyde Park, London W2 3QT
Tel (020) 7262 2325
Fax (020) 7262 0889
*www.*sasshotel.com
e-mail info@sasshotel.com

Key to Accommodation Symbols

HOTELS

l.o. Last order for evening meal.

✗ Facilities for non-smokers.

⊡ Passenger lift.

⊡ Television in all bedrooms.

♡ Tea/coffee making facilities in all bedrooms.

UL Unlicensed (alcoholic drinks not served).

✦ Conference facilities for 10 or more persons.

⇋ Garage or parking.

⬧ Ground floor bedrooms.

◗ Night porter on duty.

✆ Telephone in all bedrooms.

▣ Four poster bed(s).

▨ Indoor swimming pool.

⊨ Lounge for residents' use.

SELF CATERING

⇋ Garage or parking.

▣ Washing machine.

♠ Daily cleaning service.

⊡ Television in all units.

LP Linen provided.

◨ Ironing facilities.

▥ Central heating.

✗ Dogs not accepted.

GROUP AND YOUTH

⇋ Garage or parking.

⊡ Television lounge.

▥ Central heating.

♣ Games room.

⛻ Children welcome.

⊨ Lounge for residents' use.

☎ Public telephone.

◨ Ironing facilities.

⬧ Ground floor bedrooms.

CARAVAN AND CAMPING

⇋ Garage or parking.

LONDON TOURIST BOARD'S PHONE GUIDE

London Tourist Board's recorded information service is available 24 hours a day. It's updated daily to give you the latest information on London's events, exhibitions, theatres, places to visit, sightseeing, pageantry and much more.

Simply Dial 09064-123 plus the last three numbers as shown

WHAT'S ON
What's on this week.............................400
What's on – next 3 months 401
London parks......................................406
Christmas & Easter 418
Changing the Guard 411
Current exhibitions..............................403
Rock & pop concerts 422
Lord Mayor's Show, State Opening of
Parliament & Trooping the Colour 413

OUT & ABOUT
Travel in London..................................430
River trips/boat hire 432
Guided tours & walks..........................431
Getting to the airports 433
Shops and stores 486
Street markets 428
Eating out 485
Gay and lesbian London 09068 141120

THEATRE
West End shows...................................416
Non-West End shows...........................434

WHERE TO TAKE CHILDREN
What's on 404
Places to visit 424

PLACES TO VISIT
Museums and galleries.........................429
Palaces (inc Buckingham Palace)...........481
Attractions in Greenwich 482
Famous houses & gardens 483
Other attractions 480
Day trips from London 484

ACCOMMODATION
General advice 435

Information for callers using
push-button telephones
(020) 7971 0027. To order free cards
listing all services call (020) 7971 0026.

INFORMATION BY FAX
To receive information on the following topics dial the number you require on a fax machine. Press start/receive after the tone, or set fax machine to polling mode. After a short pause the pages will start to come through.

Major events 09068 353 715
Events in London 09068 353 716
Changing the Guard 09068 353 718
Booking a tour guide 09068 353 719
River trips schedule 09068 353 720
Shops and stores 09068 353 721
Eating out 09068 353 722

Calls charged at 60p per minute at all times (as at September 2000) plus any hotel/ payphone surcharge.

Please note that 09064/8 numbers
are not accessible outside the UK.

LONDON
Tourist Board
and Convention Bureau

Good Value Accommodation
in Central London
Central Reservations Telephone (020) 7402 0202

Abbey Court and Westpoint Hotel

- ✓ Pleasant central location
- ✓ Convenient location 2 minutes from Paddington Station & Heathrow Express, & 4 minutes from Airbus
- ✓ Easy access to all London's important tourist sights, shopping districts, theatres, Oxford Street & Piccadilly Circus
- ✓ En-Suite shower & w.c. in all rooms
- ✓ Lift to all floors
- ✓ Each room with colour T.V., radio & telephone
- ✓ Car parking by arrangement

RATES	LOW SEASON	HIGH SEASON
Singles	from £48.00	from £56.00
Doubles *pp*	from £32.00	from £37.00
Triples *pp*	from £26.00	from £28.00
Family Room *pp*	from £22.00	from £24.00

Sass House Hotel

Central London hotel located within two minutes walk from Hyde Park. Most rooms with private showers/toilets. All rooms have colour TV and radio. Easy access to all tourist attractions – within 5 minutes walking distance of Lancaster Gate and Paddington underground/mainline stations and Heathrow Express.

RATES	LOW SEASON	HIGH SEASON
Twin *pp*	from £26.00	from £29.00
Doubles *pp*	from £24.50	from £28.00
Triples *pp*	from £22.00	from £24.00
Family Room *pp*	from £19.50	from £21.50

Sass House Hotel
11 Craven Terrace,
Hyde Park, London W2 3QT
Tel (020) 7262 2325
Fax (020) 7262 0889
*www.*sasshotel.com
e-mail info@sasshotel.com

Abbey Court and Westpoint Hotel
170-174 Sussex Gardens
Hyde Park London W2 1TP
Tel (020) 7402 0704
Fax (020) 7262 2055
*www.*westpointhotel.com
e-mail info@westpointhotel.com
Tel (020) 7402 0281
Fax (020) 7224 9114
*www.*abbeycourt.com
e-mail info@abbeycourt.com

NAYLAND HOTEL
A LUXURY YOU CAN AFFORD
200 METRES FROM PADDINGTON STATION

THE HOTEL: Nayland Hotel offers exceptionally high standards of comfort and service at very competitive prices.

THE LOCATION: The Nayland is the perfect base from which to explore London. Situated in an elegant avenue near Hyde Park, Nayland provides easy access to Oxford Street, Marble Arch, Madame Tussauds, Buckingham Palace and just about anywhere one would like to go in Central London. Communications are excellent, with Paddington and Lancaster Gate underground Stations just a short walk from the Hotel.

THE ROOMS: A total of 41 Rooms provide all the comforts and private facilities one could hope for.
These include toilets & showers, direct-dial telephone, colour television, satellite television, hair dryers, radio and many more. Automatic lift to all floors.

THE FACILITIES: Our Reception Staff are at your service 24 hours a day. Traditional English Breakfast, which is included in your Room rate, is served in a bright and cheerful Dining Room. Drinks can be enjoyed in our cosy Bar or you could just relax in the beautiful surroundings of our lounge.

RATES	LOW SEASON	HIGH SEASON
Singles	from £45.00	from £59.00
Doubles *pp*	from £28.00	from £39.50
Triples & Families *pp*	from £24.00	from £33.00

132/134 Sussex Gardens, Paddington, London W2 1UB,
Tel. 020-7723 4615 (4 lines), Fax. 020-7402 3292,
Web Site: http://www.naylandhotel.com
E-MAIL: naylandhotel@easynet.co.uk

accommodation

HOTELS AND BED AND BREAKFASTS

SW1
Victoria/Westminster

Airways Hotel Nationlodge Ltd ◆◆

29-31 St George's Drive, Victoria,
London SW1V 4DG
Tel: (020) 7834 0205/
(020) 7834 3567
Fax: (020) 7932 0007
E-mail: sales@airways-hotel.com
⊖/⇄ VICTORIA
Centrally located, close to Victoria
underground, rail and coach stations
and the Gatwick Express terminal.
Bedrooms: 8 single, 9 double,
11 twin, 5 triple, 5 family
Bathrooms: 38 en suite, 1 shared
Bed & Breakfast: single £55.00-
£60.00, double £65.00-£80.00
Methods of payment: Mastercard/
Visa/Barclaycard/American Express/
JCB/Diners/Switch/Delta/Eurocheque
▫ ✿ 📞 🖳 ◗ 🖭 🎿 🚬

The Berkeley

Wilton Place, Knightsbridge, London
SW1X 7RL
Tel: (020) 7235 6000
Fax: (020) 7235 4330
E-mail: info@the_berkeley.co.uk
⊖ HYDE PARK CORNER
The elegant Berkeley in Belgravia
provides traditional service while
offering high standards of modern
comfort.
Bedrooms: 14 single, 144 double
Bathrooms: 158 en suite
Bed only: single £335.00, double
£405.00-£425.00
Evening meal: 1900 (l.o. 2245)
Parking for: 50

Methods of payment: Mastercard/
Visa/Barclaycard/American Express/
JCB/Eurocard/Diners/Eurocheque
▫ 📞 ✁ 🖳 ◗ 🖭 🎿 🚗 🖾

Carlton Hotel ◆◆

90 Belgrave Road, Victoria, London
SW1V 2BJ
Tel: (020) 7976 6634/
(020) 7932 0913
Fax: (020) 7821 8020
E-mail: cityhotelcarlton@btconnect.
com
⊖/⇄ VICTORIA
Small, friendly bed and breakfast,
situated near Victoria station and within
walking distance of Buckingham
Palace. Within easy reach of Trafalgar
Square and Piccadilly Circus.
Bedrooms: 4 single, 5 double, 2 twin,
6 triple
Bathrooms: 11 en suite, 1 shower
only, 1 shared
Bed & Breakfast: single £45.00-
£54.00, double £54.00-£64.00
Methods of payment: Mastercard/
Visa/Barclaycard/American Express/
Eurocard/Diners/Switch/Delta/
Eurocheque
▫ ✿ 📞 🖳 ◗ 🎿

Caswell Hotel ◆◆

25 Gloucester Street, London
SW1V 2DB
Tel: (020) 7834 6345
E-mail: manager@hotellondon.co.uk
⊖/⇄ VICTORIA
Pleasant, family-run hotel in a quiet
location.
Bedrooms: 2 single, 7 double, 4 twin,
2 triple, 2 family
Bathrooms: 7 en suite, 5 shared
Bed & Breakfast: single £35.00-
£60.00, double £44.00-£74.00
Methods of payment: Mastercard/
Visa/Barclaycard/JCB/Eurocard/

Switch/Delta/Eurocheque
▫ ✿ 🖳 🎿

Collin House ◆◆◆

104 Ebury Street, London
SW1W 9QD
Tel: (020) 7730 8031
Fax: (020) 7730 8031
⊖/⇄ VICTORIA
Conveniently located for Victoria rail,
underground and coach stations.
Ideal base for visiting London and
the surrounding areas.
Bedrooms: 3 single, 5 double, 4 twin,
1 triple
Bathrooms: 8 en suite, 3 shared
Bed & Breakfast: single £52.00-
£60.00, double £65.00-£78.00
Non-smoking establishment
Methods of payment: Eurocheque
🖭 ✁ 🖃 🎿

Crowne Plaza London – St James

41-54 Buckingham Gate, London
SW1E 6AF
Tel: (020) 7834 6655/
(020) 7963 8301
Fax: (020) 7630 7587
E-mail: resv@cplonsj.co.uk
⊖ ST JAMES'S PARK,
⊖/⇄ VICTORIA
Traditional hotel close to Buckingham
Palace and within easy reach of
West End and City. Self-catering
apartments also available.
Bedrooms: 165 double, 105 twin
Bathrooms: 270 en suite
Bed & Breakfast: single £246.00-
£511.00, double £262.00-£527.00
Evening meal: 1830 (l.o. 2230)
Methods of payment: Mastercard/
Visa/Barclaycard/American Express/
JCB/Eurocard/Diners/Switch/
Eurocheque
▫ ✿ 📞 ✁ 🖳 ◗ 🎿

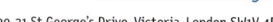

hotels & b&bs

Dolphin Square Hotel ★★★★

Dolphin Square, Chichester Street, London SW1V 3LX
Tel: (020) 7834 3800/
0800 616607
Fax: (020) 7798 8735
E-mail: reservations@dolphinsquare hotel.co.uk
⊖ **PIMLICO**
Centrally located, all-suite hotel; set among private gardens with its own extensive health and fitness spa facilities.
Bedrooms: 109 double, 10 triple, 29 family
Bathrooms: 148 en suite
Bed & Breakfast: single £142.50, double £167.50–£207.50
Evening meal: 1800 (l.o. 2230)
Parking for: 17
Methods of payment: Mastercard/ Visa/Barclaycard/American Express/ Eurocard/Diners/Switch/Delta/ Eurocheque

Dover Hotel ◆◆

44 Belgrave Road, London SW1V 1RG
Tel: (020) 7821 9085
Fax: (020) 7834 6425
E-mail: dover@rooms.demon.co.uk
⊖/≠ **VICTORIA**
Small, friendly bed and breakfast hotel within easy access of all major attractions and three minutes from Victoria station.
Bedrooms: 4 single, 9 double, 7 twin, 9 triple, 4 family
Bathrooms: 29 en suite, 4 shower only, 2 shared
Bed & Breakfast: single £40.00–£55.00, double £50.00–£70.00
Methods of payment: Mastercard/ Visa/Barclaycard/American Express/ JCB/Eurocard/Diners/Switch/Delta/ Eurocheque

The Goring Hotel
★★★★ Gold Award

15 Beeston Place, Grosvenor Gardens, London SW1W 0JW
Tel: (020) 7396 9000
Fax: (020) 7834 4393
E-mail: reception@goringhotel.co.uk
⊖/≠ **VICTORIA**

Family-owned hotel with private garden, near Buckingham Palace and parks.
Bedrooms: 20 single, 50 double, 4 twin
Bathrooms: 74 en suite, 1 shared
Bed & Breakfast: single £217.69, double £276.75–£406.00
Evening meal: 1800 (l.o. 2200)
Parking for: 7
Methods of payment: Mastercard/ Visa/Barclaycard/American Express/ Diners/Switch

The Halkin

5-6 Halkin Street, Belgravia, London SW1X 7DJ
Tel: (020) 7333 1000
Fax: (020) 7333 1100
E-mail: res@halkin.co.uk
⊖ **HYDE PARK CORNER,**
⊖/≠ **VICTORIA**
Set in a peaceful side street in Belgravia. The Halkin is a stylish and elegant, small, luxury hotel.
Bedrooms: 41 double
Bathrooms: 41 en suite
Bed & Breakfast: single £260.00–£365.00, double £260.00–£365.00
Evening meal: 1930 (l.o. 2300)
Methods of payment: Mastercard/ Visa/Barclaycard/American Express/ JCB/Eurocard/Diners/Switch/Delta

Hanover Hotel ◆◆

30-32 St George's Drive, London SW1V 4BN
Tel: (020) 7834 0367/
(020) 7834 7617
Fax: (020) 7976 5587
E-mail: reservations@hanoverhotel. co.uk
⊖/≠ **VICTORIA**
Comfortable, clean and conveniently located in central London. All rooms are en suite with tea and coffee making facilities, colour TV and direct dial telephone.
Bedrooms: 8 single, 3 double, 12 twin, 12 triple, 4 family
Bathrooms: 38 en suite, 1 shower only, 1 shared
Methods of payment: Mastercard/ Visa/Barclaycard/American Express/ JCB/Eurocard/Diners/Delta/ Eurocheque

Holiday Inn London – Victoria

2 Bridge Place, Victoria, London SW1V 1QA
Tel: (020) 7834 8123
Fax: (020) 7828 1099
⊖/≠ **VICTORIA**
Modern, Scandinavian hotel with extensive leisure facilities, located adjacent to Victoria station.
Bedrooms: 22 single, 61 double, 122 twin, 9 family
Bathrooms: 214 en suite
Bed & Breakfast: single £140.00–£215.00, double £140.00–£240.00
Evening meal: 1800 (l.o. 2230)
Methods of payment: Mastercard/ Visa/Barclaycard/American Express/ JCB/Eurocard/Diners/Switch/Delta/ Eurocheque

Huttons Hotel ◆

55 Belgrave Road, London SW1V 2BB
Tel: (020) 7834 3726
Fax: (020) 7834 3389
E-mail: reservations@hutton-hotel. co.uk
⊖/≠ **VICTORIA**
Within a few minutes' walk of Victoria train and coach stations. British Airways bus stop nearby. Recently renovated. All rooms have hot and cold water, central heating, radio, TV and telephone. Lift to all floors.
Bedrooms: 8 single, 11 double, 22 twin, 7 triple, 6 family
Bathrooms: 54 en suite, 4 shared
Methods of payment: Mastercard/ Visa/Barclaycard/American Express/ JCB/Eurocard/Diners/Switch/Delta

Hyatt Carlton Tower
★★★★★ Gold Award

Cadogan Place, London SW1X 9PY
Tel: (020) 7235 1234
Fax: (020) 7235 9129
E-mail: ctower@hytlondon.co.uk
⊖ **KNIGHTSBRIDGE**
In the heart of London's Knightsbridge shopping area, the hotel is within easy reach of the City and tourist attractions.
Bedrooms: 6 single, 117 double, 38 twin, 59 family
Bathrooms: 220 en suite

Good Value Accommodation
in Central London
Central Reservations Telephone (020) 7402 0202

Abbey Court and Westpoint Hotel

- ✓ Pleasant central location
- ✓ Convenient location 2 minutes from Paddington Station & Heathrow Express, & 4 minutes from Airbus
- ✓ Easy access to all London's important tourist sights, shopping districts, theatres, Oxford Street and Piccadilly Circus
- ✓ En-Suite shower & w.c. in all rooms

- ✓ Lift to all floors
- ✓ Each room with colour T.V., radio & telephone
- ✓ Car parking by arrangement

Abbey Court and Westpoint Hotel
170-174 Sussex Gardens
Hyde Park London W2 1TP
Tel (020) 7402 0704
Fax (020) 7262 2055
www.westpointhotel.com
e-mail info@westpointhotel.com
Tel (020) 7402 0281
Fax (020) 7224 9114
www.abbeycourt.com
e-mail info@abbeycourt.com

RATES	LOW SEASON	HIGH SEASON
Singles	from £48.00	from £56.00
Doubles *pp*	from £32.00	from £37.00
Triples *pp*	from £26.00	from £28.00
Family Room *pp*	from £22.00	from £24.00

Sass House Hotel

Central London hotel located within two minutes walk from Hyde Park. Most rooms with private showers/toilets. All rooms have colour TV and radio. Easy access to all tourist attractions – within 5 minutes walking distance of Lancaster Gate and Paddington underground/ mainline stations and Heathrow Express.

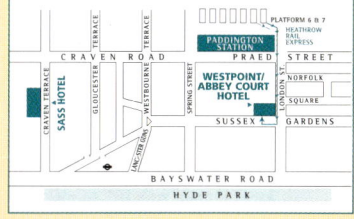

RATES	LOW SEASON	HIGH SEASON
Twin *pp*	from £26.00	from £29.00
Doubles *pp*	from £24.50	from £28.00
Triples *pp*	from £22.00	from £24.00
Family Room *pp*	from £19.50	from £21.50

Sass House Hotel
11 Craven Terrace,
Hyde Park, London W2 3QT
Tel (020) 7262 2325
Fax (020) 7262 0889
www.sasshotel.com
e-mail info@sasshotel.com

hotels & b&bs

MARBLE ARCH

Budget-priced hotel, formerly the home of the famous Victorian painter and Limerick writer, Edward Lear. One minute's walk from Oxford Street and in a very convenient central location for West End theatres and shops.
Bedrooms: 13 single, 4 double, 10 twin, 2 triple, 2 family
Bathrooms: 3 en suite, 1 private, 7 shower only, 6 shared
Methods of payment: Mastercard/Visa/Barclaycard/Eurocard/Switch/Delta/Eurocheque
□ ♢ ✆ 🖷 🖭 🕭

Four Seasons Hotel

Hamilton Place, Park Lane, London W1A 1AZ
Tel: (020) 7499 0888
Fax: (020) 7493 1895
⊖ HYDE PARK CORNER
Luxury hotel close to Hyde Park and convenient for shops and theatres.
Bedrooms: 63 single, 123 double, 34 twin
Bathrooms: 220 en suite
Bed only: single £280.00-£290.00, double £300.00-£310.00
Evening meal: 1800 (l.o. 2230)
Parking for: 55
Methods of payment: Mastercard/Visa/American Express/JCB/Eurocard/Diners/Switch/Delta/Eurocheque
□ ✆ ✗ 🖷 🕭 🚗 🕭

Glynne Court Hotel ◆◆

41 Great Cumberland Place, Marble Arch, London W1H 7LG
Tel: (020) 7262 4344
Fax: (020) 7724 2071
⊖ MARBLE ARCH
Friendly, comfortable hotel in a prime location, convenient for shops, theatres and business. Two minutes' walk from Marble Arch, Hyde Park and Oxford Street. Budget hotel in the heart of London's West End.
Bedrooms: 2 single, 6 double, 2 twin, 3 triple, 1 family
Bathrooms: 12 en suite, 3 shared
Bed & Breakfast: single £50.00-£60.00, double £55.00-£75.00
Methods of payment: Mastercard/Visa/Barclaycard/American Express/JCB/Eurocard/Diners/Switch/Delta/Eurocheque
□ ♢ ✆ 🖳 🕭 🕭

Hallam Hotel ◆◆◆

12 Hallam Street, Portland Place, London W1N 5LF
Tel: (020) 7580 1166
Fax: (020) 7323 4527
⊖ OXFORD CIRCUS
Quiet, friendly hotel five minutes from Oxford Circus.
Bedrooms: 15 single, 6 double, 4 twin
Bathrooms: 25 en suite
Bed & Breakfast: single £80.00-£95.00, double £80.00-£97.50
Methods of payment: Mastercard/Visa/Barclaycard/American Express/Eurocard/Diners/Eurocheque
□ ♢ ✆ ✗ 🖷 🕭 🕭

Hotel Inter-Continental London

1 Hamilton Place, Hyde Park Corner, London W1V 0QY
Tel: (020) 7409 3131
Fax: (020) 7493 3476
E-mail: london@interconti.com
⊖ HYDE PARK CORNER
In the heart of London, on Hyde Park Corner. Close to Piccadilly, West End shopping and theatres.
Bedrooms: 281 double, 124 twin
Bathrooms: 405 en suite, 3 shared
Bed only: single £295.00, double £295.00
Evening meal: 1800 (l.o. 2300)
Parking for: 100
Methods of payment: Mastercard/Visa/Barclaycard/American Express/Eurocard/Diners/Switch/Delta/Eurocheque
□ ♢ ✆ ✗ 🖷 🕭 🚗 🕭

Hotel La Place APPLIED

17 Nottingham Place, London W1M 3FF
Tel: (020) 7486 2323
Fax: (020) 7486 4335
E-mail: reservations@hotellaplace.com
⊖ BAKER STREET
West End hotel specialising in personal service and friendliness. Multilingual staff. Caters especially for women travelling alone.
Bedrooms: 5 single, 3 double, 6 twin, 3 triple, 3 family
Bathrooms: 20 en suite
Bed & Breakfast: single £95.00-£150.00, double £115.00-£170.00

Evening meal: 1800 (l.o. 2030)
Methods of payment: Mastercard/Visa/Barclaycard/American Express/JCB/Eurocard/Diners/Switch/Delta/Eurocheque
□ ♢ ✆ 🖷 🕭 🚗 🕭 🍴

Kenwood House Hotel ◆

114 Gloucester Place, London W1H 3DB
Tel: (020) 7935 3473/
(020) 7935 9455
Fax: (020) 7224 0582
E-mail: kenwoodhouse@yahoo.co.uk
⊖ BAKER STREET
A small, friendly bed and breakfast hotel in a central location, with budget prices.
Bedrooms: 4 single, 6 double, 4 twin, 2 family
Bathrooms: 11 en suite, 4 shared
Bed & Breakfast: single £30.00-£50.00, double £50.00-£70.00
Methods of payment: Mastercard/Visa/Barclaycard/American Express/Eurocard/Diners/Switch/Delta/Eurocheque
□ 🖭 🕭 🚗 🕭 🍴

Le Meridien Grosvenor House ★★★★★

Park Lane, London W1A 3AA
Tel: 0870 400 8500
Fax: (020) 7493 3341
E-mail: grosvenor.reservations@forte-hotels.com
⊖ MARBLE ARCH/HYDE PARK CORNER
This famous hotel is situated on Park Lane overlooking the 360 acres of Hyde Park.
Bedrooms: 75 single, 113 double, 176 twin, 73 triple
Bathrooms: 437 en suite
Bed only: single £267.00, double £287.00
Evening meal: 1800 (l.o. 2245)
Parking for: 120
Methods of payment: Mastercard/Visa/Barclaycard/American Express/JCB/Diners/Switch
□ ♢ ✆ ✗ 🖷 🕭 🚗 🍴 🕭 🔲

Le Meridien Piccadilly
★★★★★ Silver Award

21 Piccadilly, London W1V 0BH
Tel: 0870 400 8400
Fax: (020) 7437 3574
E-mail: lmpiccres@forte-hotels.com

hotels & b&bs

➍ PICCADILLY CIRCUS
Traditional, centrally located hotel with a unique leisure club and high standards of service and facilities.
Bedrooms: 71 single, 111 double, 49 twin, 35 family
Bathrooms: 266 en suite
Evening meal: 1900 (l.o. 2230)
Methods of payment: Mastercard/ Visa/Barclaycard/American Express/ JCB/Eurocard/Diners/Switch/Delta/ Eurocheque
□ 📞 ⚒ 🅿 🅾 🖃 🐕 🍽

The Langham Hilton

1c Portland Place, Regent Street, London W1N 4JA
Tel: (020) 7636 1000
Fax: (020) 7323 2340
E-mail: rm_langham@hilton.com
➍ OXFORD CIRCUS
A revival of London's first grand hotel restored to its Victorian splendour. The Langham Hilton overlooks Portland Place and Regent's Park and is five minutes from Oxford Street.
Bedrooms: 285 double, 94 twin
Bathrooms: 379 en suite
Bed & Breakfast: single £388.04-£1,813.00, double £412.13-£1,837.11
Evening meal: 1800 (l.o. 2245)
Methods of payment: Mastercard/ Visa/Barclaycard/American Express/ JCB/Diners/Switch/Delta
□ 📞 ⚒ 🅾 🍽

The Leonard
★ ★ ★ ★ Townhouse Gold Award

15 Seymour Street, London W1H 5AA
Tel: (020) 7935 2010
Fax: (020) 7935 6700
E-mail: the.leonard@dial.pipex.com
➍ MARBLE ARCH
Four 18th-century townhouses, elegantly restored. Twenty suites and eight bedrooms, all with air-conditioning, 24-hour room service and friendly staff.
Bedrooms: 24 double, 1 triple, 3 family
Bathrooms: 28 en suite
Bed & Breakfast: single £228.50-£604.50, double £269.00-£621.50
Evening meal: 1500 (l.o. 2300)
Methods of payment: Mastercard/ Visa/Barclaycard/American Express/ JCB/Diners/Switch/Eurocheque
□ 🌣 📞 ⚒ 🅾 🖃 🛄 🍽

Lincoln House Hotel ◆◆

33 Gloucester Place, London W1H 3PD
Tel: (020) 7486 7630
Fax: (020) 7486 0166
E-mail: reservations@lincoln-house-hotel.co.uk
➍ MARBLE ARCH
Recently refurbished Georgian hotel. En suite rooms with modern comforts. Located in the heart of London, near Oxford Street shopping area and close to theatreland.
Bedrooms: 6 single, 8 double, 4 twin, 3 triple, 1 family
Bathrooms: 20 en suite, 2 private, 1 shared
Bed & Breakfast: single £65.00-£69.00, double £79.00-£99.00
Methods of payment: Mastercard/ Visa/Barclaycard/American Express/ JCB/Eurocard/Diners/Switch/Delta
□ 🌣 📞 🅾 🖃

London Hilton
★ ★ ★ ★ ★ Silver Award

22 Park Lane, London W1Y 4BE
Tel: (020) 7493 8000
Fax: (020) 7208 4136
E-mail: sales_park_lane@hilton.com
➍ HYDE PARK CORNER
Built in 1963, this is the flagship hotel of Hilton International. All bedrooms have magnificent views of London. The hotel has one of the largest ballrooms in London, three restaurants and four bars.
Bedrooms: 270 double, 124 twin, 55 family
Bathrooms: 449 en suite
Bed only: single £400.00, double £400.00
Evening meal: 1900 (l.o. 2330)
Parking for: 300
Methods of payment: Mastercard/ Visa/Barclaycard/American Express/ JCB/Eurocard/Diners/Switch/Delta/ Eurocheque
□ 📞 ⚒ 🅾 🍽 🚗

London Marriott Hotel Grosvenor Square

10-13 Duke Street, London W1A 4AW
Tel: (020) 7493 1232
Fax: (020) 7491 3201
➍ BOND STREET
In the heart of Mayfair. Close to shopping, theatres, art galleries, antique shops, restaurants and Hyde Park.
Bedrooms: 2 single, 116 double, 86 twin, 17 triple
Bathrooms: 221 en suite
Evening meal: 1730 (l.o. 2200)
Parking for: 50
Methods of payment: Mastercard/ Visa/Barclaycard/American Express/ JCB/Diners/Switch/Delta/Eurocheque
□ 🌣 📞 ⚒ 🅾 🍽 🚗

London Marriott Hotel – Marble Arch

134 George Street, London W1H 6DN
Tel: (020) 7723 1277
Fax: (020) 7402 0666
➍ MARBLE ARCH
Located centrally, a short walk from Oxford Street, Hyde Park and Marble Arch underground. Paddington station is a mile away, giving access to Heathrow via the Heathrow Express.
Bedrooms: 145 double, 95 twin
Bathrooms: 240 en suite
Evening meal: 1700 (l.o. 2230)
Parking for: 80
Methods of payment: Mastercard/ Visa/Barclaycard/American Express/ JCB/Eurocard/Diners/Switch/Delta
□ 🌣 📞 ⚒ 🅾 🍽 🚗

London Mews Hilton

2 Stanhope Row, Park Lane, London W1Y 7HE
Tel: (020) 7493 7222
Fax: (020) 7629 9423
E-mail: lonmwtwgm@hilton.com
➍ GREEN PARK
An intimate townhouse hotel situated in the heart of Mayfair. Close to Piccadilly, Oxford Street and many major attractions. Direct link to Heathrow.
Bedrooms: 19 single, 32 double, 20 twin
Bathrooms: 71 en suite
Bed & Breakfast: single £159.00-£184.00, double £159.00-£184.00
Evening meal: 1730 (l.o. 2130)
Parking for: 4
Methods of payment: Mastercard/ Visa/Barclaycard/American Express/ JCB/Eurocard/Diners/Switch/Delta/ Eurocheque
□ 🌣 📞 ⚒ 🅾 🍽 🚗

Marble Arch Inn ◆◆

49-50 Upper Berkeley Street,
Marble Arch, London W1H 7PN
Tel: (020) 7723 7888
Fax: (020) 7723 6060
E-mail: marble@rooms.demon.co.uk
⊖ **MARBLE ARCH**
Friendly hotel located near Marble
Arch, within minutes of Hyde Park
and Oxford Street and within easy
reach of other major attractions.
Bedrooms: 2 single, 8 double, 9 twin,
6 triple, 4 family
Bathrooms: 25 en suite, 4 shower
only, 2 shared
Bed & Breakfast: single £30.00-
£60.00, double £40.00-£70.00
Methods of payment: Mastercard/
Visa/Barclaycard/American Express/
JCB/Eurocard/Diners/Switch/Delta/
Eurocheque
□ ✿ ℃ ▥ ✕ ◑ ♨ ⛟

May Fair Inter-Continental London ★★★★★

Stratton Street, London W1A 2AN
Tel: (020) 7629 7777
Fax: (020) 7629 1459
E-mail: mayfair@interconti.com
⊖ **GREEN PARK**
Situated close to Green Park and
Piccadilly. Facilities include informal
restaurant, May Fair cafe, May Fair
theatre, crystal ballroom, spa health
club, business centre and two bars.
Bedrooms: 79 single, 163 double,
45 twin
Bathrooms: 287 en suite
Bed & Breakfast: single £385.00,
double £420.00
Evening meal: 1900 (l.o. 2230)
Methods of payment: Mastercard/
Visa/Barclaycard/American Express/
JCB/Eurocard/Diners/Switch/Delta/
Eurocheque
□ ✿ ℃ ▤ ◑ ♨ ⛟ ▦

The Metropolitan

Old Park Lane, London W1Y 4LB
Tel: (020) 7447 1000
Fax: (020) 7447 1100
E-mail: res@metropolitan.co.uk
⊖ **HYDE PARK CORNER**
The Metropolitan is contemporary in
style and attracts a fashionable
market. Nobu, the Japanese
restaurant and the chic Met Bar are
on-site.
Bedrooms: 59 single, 96 double

Bathrooms: 155 en suite
Bed & Breakfast: single £283.25-
£1,663.00, double £325.63-£2,092.25
Parking for: 20
Methods of payment: Mastercard/
Visa/Barclaycard/American Express/
JCB/Diners/Switch/Delta/Eurocheque
□ ℃ ✕ ▤ ◑ ♨ ⛟

Millennium Britannia Mayfair

Grosvenor Square, London W1A 3AN
Tel: (020) 7629 9400
Fax: (020) 7629 7736
E-mail: britannia.res@mill-cop.com
⊖ **BOND STREET**
Located in the picturesque Grosvenor
Square in Mayfair, offering traditional
British hospitality with unobtrusive
yet friendly service. Conveniently
situated for the historic sites, London
theatreland and prime shopping
areas.
Bedrooms: 23 single, 200 double,
90 twin
Bathrooms: 313 en suite
Evening meal: 1830 (l.o. 2230)
Parking for: 210
Methods of payment: Mastercard/
Visa/Barclaycard/American Express/
JCB/Diners
□ ℃ ✕ ▤ ◑ ♨ ⛟

Park Lane Hotel
★★★★★ Silver Award

Piccadilly, London W1Y 8BX
Tel: (020) 7499 6321
Fax: (020) 7499 1965
E-mail: reservations_centrallondon@
sheraton.com
⊖ **GREEN PARK**
Highly commended hotel on
Piccadilly overlooking Green Park
towards Buckingham Palace, offering
good service and modern facilities.
Bedrooms: 37 single, 129 double,
100 twin, 39 family
Bathrooms: 305 en suite
Bed only: single £323.13, double
£346.63
Evening meal: 1900 (l.o. 2300)
Parking for: 150
Methods of payment: Mastercard/
Visa/Barclaycard/American Express/
JCB/Eurocard/Diners/Eurocheque
□ ℃ ✕ ▤ ◑ ♨ ⛟

Posthouse Regent's Park

Carburton Street, London W1P 8EE
Tel: (020) 7388 2300

Fax: (020) 7387 2806
⊖ **GREAT PORTLAND STREET**
Situated just north of Oxford Street
and to the east of Regent Street,
close to Regent's Park and London
Zoo. Business services available.
Bedrooms: 3 single, 205 double,
118 twin
Bathrooms: 326 en suite
Bed & Breakfast: single £148.00-
£177.45, double £160.55-£181.55
Evening meal: 1800 (l.o. 2200)
Parking for: 80
Methods of payment: Mastercard/
Visa/Barclaycard/American Express/
JCB/Eurocard/Diners/Switch/Delta/
Eurocheque
□ ✿ ℃ ✕ ▤ ◑ ♒ ♨ ⛟

Prince Regent Hotel ◆◆

37 Nottingham Place, London
W1M 3FE
Tel: (020) 7935 4276/
(020) 7487 5153
Fax: (020) 7224 1582
E-mail: princerh@ukonline.co.uk
⊖ **BAKER STREET**
In the heart of London's West End,
yet in a quiet position. Ideal for
people coming to Harley Street
hospitals and clinics.
Bedrooms: 7 single, 4 double,
5 twin, 4 triple
Bathrooms: 20 en suite
Bed and breakfast: single £55.00-
£60.00, double £70.00-£80.00
Methods of payment: Mastercard/
Visa/Barclaycard/American Express/
JCB/Diners/Switch/Delta
□ ℃ ▤ ◑ ♨ ♒ ♨

Radisson Edwardian Berkshire Hotel

350 Oxford Street, London W1N 0BY
Tel: (020) 7629 7474
Fax: (020) 7629 8156
E-mail: jahanbas@radissonedwardian.
com
⊖ **BOND STREET**
A traditional boutique hotel ideally
situated in central London, easily
accessible for businessmen and
leisure travellers alike.
Bedrooms: 48 single, 79 double,
20 twin
Bathrooms: 147 en suite
Bed & Breakfast: single £159.00-
£229.00, double £189.00-£249.00
Evening meal: 1730 (l.o. 2300)

hotels & b&bs

Non-smoking establishment
Methods of payment: Mastercard/
Visa/Barclaycard/JCB/Eurocard/
Diners/Switch/Delta/Eurocheque
▢ ✿ ☎ ⌨ ▤ ◖ ⊨ ♨ ☂

Radisson Edwardian Grafton Hotel

130 Tottenham Court Road, London
W1P 9HP
Tel: (020) 7388 4131/
(020) 7387 3565
Fax: (020) 7753 0334
E-mail: resgraf@radisson.com
✈ **WARREN STREET**
A traditional hotel close to the City
and the West End. Over 300
Edwardian-inspired rooms, with
excellent facilities.
Bedrooms: 82 single, 119 double,
98 twin, 25 triple
Bathrooms: 324 en suite
Evening meal: 1700 (l.o. 2230)
Methods of payment: Mastercard/
Visa/American Express/Diners/Switch
▢ ✿ ☎ ⌨ ▤ ◖

Radisson Edwardian Savoy Court

19-25 Granville Place, London
W1H 0EH
Tel: (020) 7408 0130
Fax: (020) 7493 2070
✈ **MARBLE ARCH**
In a quiet location just off Oxford
Street at Marble Arch. The hotel
provides traditional elegance at
reasonable cost.
Bedrooms: 32 single, 30 double,
24 twin, 13 triple
Bathrooms: 99 en suite
Evening meal: 1700 (l.o. 2130)
Methods of payment: Mastercard/
Visa/Barclaycard/American Express/
JCB/Eurocard/Diners/Switch/Delta
▢ ✿ ☎ ⌨ ▤ ◖ ☂

Radisson SAS Portman

22 Portman Square, London
W1H 9FL
Tel: (020) 7208 6000
Fax: (020) 7208 6001
E-mail: sales@lonza.rdsas.com
✈ **MARBLE ARCH**
Modern hotel situated in the heart of
London's West End with easy access
to the business and entertainment
centres. There are tennis courts in
nearby Portman Square.

Bedrooms: 17 single, 156 double,
100 twin, 7 family
Bathrooms: 280 en suite
Bed & Breakfast: single £235.00-
£470.00, double £265.00-£520.00
Evening meal: 1730 (l.o. 2300)
Parking for: 400
Methods of payment: Mastercard/
Visa/Barclaycard/American Express/
JCB/Eurocard/Diners/Switch/Delta
▢ ✿ ☎ ⌨ ▤ ◖ ⊨ ☂ ⊕

Rathbone Hotel

Rathbone Street, London W1P 2LB
Tel: (020) 7636 2001
Fax: (020) 7580 5546
E-mail: rathbonehotel@dial.pipex.com
✈ **GOODGE STREET**
Excellent location just a few minutes'
walk from Oxford Street and close to
all central London attractions. First-
class, well-appointed hotel.
Bedrooms: 17 single, 41 double,
10 twin
Bathrooms: 68 en suite
Bed & Breakfast: single £180.00-
£190.00, double £210.00-£220.00
Methods of payment: Mastercard/
Visa/Barclaycard/American Express/
JCB/Eurocard/Diners/Switch/Delta
▢ ✿ ☎ ⌨ ▤ ◖ ⊨ ☂

The Ritz Hotel

150 Piccadilly, London W1V 9DG
Tel: (020) 7493 8181
Fax: (020) 7493 2687
E-mail: enquire@theritzhotel.co.uk
✈ **GREEN PARK**
A symbol of consummate hospitality
since 1906, this international hotel is
ideally situated for shopping,
business and cultural activities.
Bedrooms: 17 single, 58 double,
55 twin
Bathrooms: 130 en suite
Bed & Breakfast: single £650.50-
£722.16, double £735.00-£816.80
Evening meal: 1830 (l.o. 2245)
Methods of payment: Mastercard/
Visa/Barclaycard/American Express/
JCB/Eurocard/Diners/Switch/Delta
▢ ☎ ▤ ◖ ⊨ ☂

Saint Georges Hotel

Langham Place, Regent Street,
London W1N 8QS
Tel: (020) 7580 0111
Fax: (020) 7436 7997

E-mail: stgeorgeshotel@talk21.com
✈ **OXFORD CIRCUS**
Modern hotel. Restaurant with
panoramic views. Spacious rooms
with bright décor and natural light.
Bedrooms: 3 single, 31 double,
52 twin
Bathrooms: 86 en suite
Bed & Breakfast: single £104.00-
£183.00
Evening meal: 1900 (l.o. 2200)
Parking for: 2
Methods of payment: Mastercard/
Visa/Barclaycard/American Express/
JCB/Eurocard/Diners/Switch/Delta/
Eurocheque
▢ ✿ ☎ ⌨ ▤ ◖ ⊨ ☂ ⊕

The Selfridge, A Thistle Hotel

Orchard Street, London W1H 0JS
Tel: (020) 7408 2080
Fax: (020) 7629 8849
E-mail: markbarrett@thistle.co.uk
✈ **BOND STREET**
One of London's most central hotels
in the heart of the West End, ideal
for nightlife and with the shopping
areas of Bond Street and Oxford
Street nearby.
Bedrooms: 86 single, 62 double,
146 twin
Bathrooms: 294 en suite
Bed only: single £187.00, double
£210.00
Evening meal: 1800 (l.o. 2300)
Methods of payment: Mastercard/
Visa/Barclaycard/American Express/
JCB/Eurocard/Diners/Switch/Delta/
Eurocheque
▢ ✿ ☎ ⌨ ▤ ◖ ⊨ ☂

Shaftesbury Avenue Hotel

65-73 Shaftesbury Avenue, London
W1V 7AA
Tel: (020) 7434 4200
Fax: (020) 7437 1717
✈ **PICCADILLY CIRCUS**
In the heart of the West End.
Centrally located for London's visitor
attractions, theatreland, nightlife and
shops. Fully refurbished during the
1999 to 2000 winter season.
Bedrooms: 6 single, 48 double,
8 twin
Bathrooms: 62 en suite
Bed & Breakfast: single £115.00-
£155.00, double £155.00-£195.00
Evening meal: 1830 (l.o. 2230)

Methods of payment: Mastercard/
Visa/Barclaycard/American Express/
Diners/Switch/Delta/Eurocheque
⌑ ✿ ↳ ⚒ ▣ ◑

Sherlock Holmes Hotel

108 Baker Street, London W1M 2LJ
Tel: (020) 7486 6161
Fax: (020) 7486 0884
E-mail: lonshafgm@hilton.com
⊖ **BAKER STREET**
Well located for shopping in Oxford
Street and Regent Street, and only
200 yards from Baker Street
underground station and Madame
Tussaud's.
Bedrooms: 14 single, 46 double,
48 twin, 5 triple, 12 family
Bathrooms: 125 en suite
Bed & Breakfast: single £95.00-
£169.00, double £107.00-£181.00
Evening meal: 1900 (l.o. 2130)
Methods of payment: Mastercard/
Visa/Barclaycard/American Express/
JCB/Eurocard/Diners/Switch/Delta/
Eurocheque
⌑ ✿ ↳ ⚒ ▣ ◑ ⏐

Ten Manchester Street ◆◆◆◆

10 Manchester Street, London
W1M 5PG
Tel: (020) 7486 6669
Fax: (020) 7224 0348
⊖ **BAKER STREET**
A discreet boutique property in the
West End, offering stylish
accommodation, a fantastic
breakfast and great value for money.
Bedrooms: 5 single, 13 double,
19 twin, 9 triple
Bathrooms: 46 en suite
Bed & Breakfast: single £120.00,
double £150.00
Methods of payment: Mastercard/
Visa/Barclaycard/American Express/
Eurocard/Switch/Delta
⌑ ✿ ↳ ⚒ ▣ ◑ ⊟ ⛊

Thistle Marble Arch

Bryanston Street, Marble Arch,
London W1A 4UR
Tel: (020) 7629 8040
Fax: (020) 7499 7792
E-mail: marble.arch@thistle.co.uk
⊖ **MARBLE ARCH**
In the heart of London's busy West
End, overlooking Oxford Street; close
to shops, theatres and nightclubs.

Bedrooms: 35 single, 153 double,
359 twin, 54 triple, 88 family
Bathrooms: 689 en suite
Bed only: single £110.00-£218.90,
double £110.00-£218.90
Evening meal: 1800 (l.o. 2100)
Methods of payment: Mastercard/
Visa/Barclaycard/American Express/
JCB/Eurocard/Diners/Switch/Delta/
Eurocheque
⌑ ✿ ↳ ⚒ ▣ ◑ ⊟ ⏐

Thistle Piccadilly

39 Coventry Street, London W1V 7FH
Tel: (020) 7930 4033
Fax: (020) 7925 2586
E-mail: piccadilly@thistle.co.uk
⊖ **LEICESTER SQUARE**
Just yards from Piccadilly Circus.
Close to Regent Street, theatres, the
National Gallery and opposite
Leicester Square.
Bedrooms: 15 single, 27 double,
44 twin, 5 triple
Bathrooms: 91 en suite
Bed only: single £155.00-£177.00,
double £188.00-£207.00
Methods of payment: Mastercard/
Visa/Barclaycard/American Express/
JCB/Eurocard/Diners/Switch/Delta/
Eurocheque
⌑ ✿ ↳ ⚒ ▣ ◑ ⊟ ⏐

Wigmore Court Hotel ◆◆◆

23 Gloucester Place, Portman
Square, London W1H 3PB
Tel: (020) 7935 0928
Fax: (020) 7487 4254
E-mail: info@wigmore-court-hotel.
co.uk
⊖ **MARBLE ARCH**
Small, clean, family-run bed and
breakfast hotel with large en suite
rooms. Three minutes' walk to
Oxford Street and Marble Arch
underground station. Competitively
priced and ideal for families.
Bedrooms: 5 single, 7 double, 3
twin, 2 triple, 1 family
Bathrooms: 16 en suite, 1 shared
Bed & Breakfast: single £40.00-
£77.00, double £75.00-£97.00
Methods of payment: Mastercard/
Visa/Barclaycard/JCB/Switch/Delta
⌑ ✿ ↳ ▥ ◑ ⊟ ⛊ ▦

Wyndham Hotel ◆◆◆

30 Wyndham Street, London
W1H 1DD

hotels & b&bs

Tel: (020) 7723 7204/
(020) 7723 9400
Fax: (020) 7724 2893
E-mail: wyndhamhotel@talk21.com
⊖/⇄ **MARYLEBONE,**
⊖ **BAKER STREET**
A small, family-run bed and
breakfast within walking distance of
Oxford Street. Refurbished in
February 2000.
Bedrooms: 4 single, 3 double,
3 twin, 1 triple
Bathrooms: 11 shower only
Methods of payment: Mastercard/
Visa/Switch/Eurocheque
⌑ ✿ ↳ ▥ ◑ ⛊

WC1/WC2
Bloomsbury/Strand/
Leicester Square

Academy Hotel ★★★

17-25 Gower Street, London
WC1E 6HG
Tel: (020) 7631 4115
Fax: (020) 7636 3442
E-mail: academyh@aol.com
⊖ **GOODGE STREET**
Charming hotel in a group of five
original Georgian townhouses in the
heart of Bloomsbury. With an award-
winning in-house restaurant,
Alchemy.
Bedrooms: 13 single, 27 double,
8 twin
Bathrooms: 48 en suite, 1 shared
Evening meal: 1800 (l.o. 2300)
Methods of payment: Mastercard/
Visa/Barclaycard/American Express/
JCB/Eurocard/Diners/Switch/Delta/
Eurocheque
⌑ ✿ ↳ ▥ ◑ ⊟ ⛊ ⏐

Blooms Townhouse
Hotel ★★★★ Townhouse

7 Montague Street, London
WC1B 5BP
Tel: (020) 7323 1717
Fax: (020) 7636 6498
E-mail: blooms@mermaid.co.uk
⊖ **RUSSELL SQUARE**
Blooms is an elegant Georgian
townhouse hotel set in the heart of
literary Bloomsbury, close to many
tourist attractions, theatreland and
Oxford Street.
Bedrooms: 5 single, 13 double,
9 twin

hotels & b&bs

Bathrooms: 27 en suite
Bed & Breakfast: single £130.00-£175.00, double £195.00-£205.00
Evening meal: 1730 (l.o. 2200)
Methods of payment: Mastercard/Visa/Barclaycard/American Express/JCB/Eurocard/Diners/Switch/Delta

Bloomsbury Park Hotel

126 Southampton Row, London WC1B 5AD
Tel: (020) 7430 0434
Fax: (020) 7242 0665
⊖/⇌ EUSTON,
⊖ RUSSELL SQUARE
Midway between the West End and the City and close to Covent Garden and the British Museum, the hotel is convenient for Euston, St Pancras and King's Cross stations.
Bedrooms: 5 single, 44 double, 46 twin
Bathrooms: 95 en suite
Evening meal: 1800 (l.o. 2130)
Methods of payment: Mastercard/Visa/Barclaycard/American Express/Diners/Switch/Delta/Eurocheque

The Bonnington in Bloomsbury ★★★

92 Southampton Row, London WC1B 4BH
Tel: (020) 7242 2828
Fax: (020) 7831 9170
E-mail: sales@bonnington.com
⊖ HOLBORN/RUSSELL SQUARE
The Bonnington is situated between the City and West End and is close to train stations and on the bus routes to Heathrow.
Bedrooms: 109 single, 44 double, 45 twin, 17 triple
Bathrooms: 215 en suite
Bed & Breakfast: single £46.00-£120.00, double £120.00-£150.00
Evening meal: 1730 (l.o. 2230)
Methods of payment: Mastercard/Visa/Barclaycard/American Express/JCB/Eurocard/Diners/Switch/Delta/Eurocheque

Country Inn Suites

110 Great Russell Street, London WC1B 3NA
Tel: (020) 7637 7777
Fax: (020) 7436 1142

⊖ TOTTENHAM COURT ROAD
Country house style hotel conveniently located for the British Museum and the West End.
Bedrooms: 12 single, 10 double, 16 twin
Bathrooms: 38 en suite
Evening meal: 1800 (l.o. 2130)
Methods of payment: Mastercard/Visa/Barclaycard/American Express/JCB/Eurocard/Diners/Switch/Delta/Eurocheque

Crescent Hotel ◆◆◆

49-50 Cartwright Gardens, Bloomsbury, London WC1H 9EL
Tel: (020) 7387 1515
Fax: (020) 7383 2054
E-mail: general.enquiries@crescenthoteloflondon.com
⊖ RUSSELL SQUARE,
⊖/⇌ EUSTON
Comfortable Georgian townhouse, in a quiet crescent, with private gardens and tennis courts.
Bedrooms: 12 single, 2 double, 3 twin, 7 triple, 3 family
Bathrooms: 18 en suite, 3 shower only, 4 shared
Bed & Breakfast: single £43.00-£70.00, double £80.00-£84.00
Methods of payment: Mastercard/Visa/Barclaycard/Eurocard/Delta/Eurocheque

Euro Hotel ◆◆◆

53 Cartwright Gardens, London WC1H 9EL
Tel: (020) 7387 4321
Fax: (020) 7383 5044
E-mail: reception@eurohotel.co.uk
⊖ RUSSELL SQUARE
Centrally located hotel close to the West End and British Museum.
Bedrooms: 8 single, 6 double, 10 twin, 7 triple, 4 family
Bathrooms: 10 en suite, 11 shared
Bed & Breakfast: single £48.00-£70.00, double £67.00-£87.00
Methods of payment: Mastercard/Visa/Barclaycard/American Express/Switch/Delta/Eurocheque

George Hotel ◆◆◆

58-60 Cartwright Gardens, London WC1H 9EL
Tel: (020) 7387 8777

Fax: (020) 7387 8666
E-mail: ghotel@aol.com
⊖ RUSSELL SQUARE
Traditional English bed and breakfast hotel in a quiet central location. Convenient for the West End and British Museum.
Bedrooms: 15 single, 5 double, 6 twin, 12 triple, 2 family
Bathrooms: 14 en suite, 2 shower only, 12 shared
Bed & Breakfast: single £49.50-£75.00, double £69.50-£90.00
Methods of payment: Mastercard/Visa/Barclaycard/Eurocard/Switch/Delta/Eurocheque

Gower House Hotel ◆

57 Gower Street, London WC1E 6HJ
Tel: (020) 7636 4685
Fax: (020) 7636 4685
⊖ GOODGE STREET
Friendly bed and breakfast hotel within easy walking distance of the British Museum, shops, theatres and restaurants.
Bedrooms: 4 single, 2 double, 6 twin, 3 triple, 1 family
Bathrooms: 3 en suite, 3 shared
Bed & Breakfast: single £40.00-£42.00, double £50.00-£52.00
Methods of payment: Mastercard/Visa/Barclaycard/JCB/Eurocard/Switch/Eurocheque

Hotel Russell

Russell Square, London WC1B 5BE
Tel: (020) 7837 6470
Fax: (020) 7837 2857
E-mail: sales.russell@principalhotels.co.uk
⊖ RUSSELL SQUARE
Facing Russell Square and close to the British Museum. Underground station nearby offering a direct service to the West End and Heathrow. Prices are subject to change.
Bedrooms: 107 single, 97 double, 103 twin, 22 triple
Bathrooms: 329 en suite
Bed & Breakfast: single £164.05-£251.95, double £225.90-£285.90
Evening meal: 1800 (l.o. 2230)
Methods of payment: Mastercard/Visa/Barclaycard/American Express/Diners/Switch/Delta

Le Meridien Waldorf
★★★★★ Silver Award

Aldwych, London WC2B 4DD
Tel: 0870 400 8484
Fax: (020) 7836 7244
➤ COVENT GARDEN
The Waldorf Meridien, located in
London's theatreland, has 292 air-
conditioned bedrooms, two
restaurants, two bars and 14
conference suites.
Bedrooms: 110 single, 151 double,
31 twin
Bathrooms: 292 en suite
Bed & Breakfast: single £320.00-
£340.00, double £340.00-£360.00
Evening meal: 1800 (l.o. 2315)
Methods of payment: Mastercard/
Visa/Barclaycard/American Express/
JCB/Diners/Switch/Delta/Eurocheque

London Ryan Hotel

Gwynne Place, King's Cross Road,
King's Cross, London WC1X 9QN
Tel: (020) 7278 2480
Fax: (020) 7837 3776
E-mail: london.ryan@thistle.co.uk
➤/≋ KING'S CROSS
Modern hotel with parking facilities.
Well situated for visiting the City and
the West End.
Bedrooms: 30 single, 117 double,
46 twin, 18 triple
Bathrooms: 211 en suite
Bed only: single £89.00-£108.00,
double £110.00-£121.00
Evening meal: 1800 (l.o. 2200)
Parking for: 26
Methods of payment: Mastercard/
Visa/Barclaycard/American Express/
JCB/Eurocard/Diners/Switch/Delta/
Eurocheque

The Montague on the Gardens ★★★★ Silver Award

15 Montague Street, Bloomsbury,
London WC1B 5BJ
Tel: (020) 7637 1001
Fax: (020) 7637 2516
E-mail: sales@montague.red
carnationhotels.com
➤/≋ EUSTON,
➤ RUSSELL SQUARE
The hotel is a Georgian-style,
traditional townhouse, centrally but
quietly located within walking
distance of Covent Garden, Oxford
Street and theatres. Opposite the
British Museum. Close to the City.
Bedrooms: 26 single, 35 double,
32 twin
Bathrooms: 93 en suite, 1 shared
Evening meal: 1730 (l.o. 2300)
Methods of payment: Mastercard/
Visa/Barclaycard/American Express/
JCB/Eurocard/Diners

myhotel Bloomsbury APPLIED

11-13 Bayley Street, Bedford Square,
London WC1B 3HD
Tel: (020) 7667 6000
Fax: (020) 7667 6044
E-mail: guest_services@myhotels.
co.uk
➤ TOTTENHAM COURT ROAD
The hotel has meeting and private
dining facilities, a library which is a
peaceful sanctuary, a health studio,
76 well-appointed rooms and suites,
a restaurant and a champagne bar.
Designed by the Conran Design
Partnership.
Bedrooms: 18 single, 50 double,
8 twin
Bathrooms: 76 en suite, 2 shared
Bed & Breakfast: single £193.88-
£217.38, double £240.88-£264.38
Evening meal: 1800 (l.o. 2300)
Methods of payment: Mastercard/
Visa/Barclaycard/American Express/
Eurocard/Diners/Switch/Delta/
Eurocheque

One Aldwych

1 Aldwych, London WC2B 4BZ
Tel: (020) 7300 1000
Fax: (020) 7300 1001
E-mail: sales@onealdwych.co.uk
➤/≋ CHARING CROSS
One Aldwych was created in one of
the most important Edwardian
buildings in London. The original
architects, Mewes and Davis, were
also responsible for the Ritz Hotel in
Paris and RAC Club in London.
Bedrooms: 105 double
Bathrooms: 105 en suite
Bed only: single £299.63-£364.25,
double £323.13-£387.75
Evening meal: 1800 (l.o. 2315)
Methods of payment: Mastercard/
Visa/Barclaycard/American Express/
JCB/Diners/Switch/Delta

Posthouse Bloomsbury ★★★

Coram Street, London WC1N 1HT
Tel: 0870 400 9222
Fax: (020) 7837 5374
E-mail: hgb1261@forte-hotels.com
➤ RUSSELL SQUARE
Modern hotel. Ideally located for
theatreland, shopping and the City.
Bedrooms: 135 single, 60 double,
59 twin, 30 family
Bathrooms: 284 en suite
Bed & Breakfast: single £99.00-
£159.00, double £128.00-£169.00
Evening meal: 1800 (l.o. 2200)
Parking for: 201
Methods of payment: Mastercard/
Visa/Barclaycard/American Express/
JCB/Eurocard/Diners/Switch/Delta/
Eurocheque

Radisson Edwardian Hampshire Hotel
★★★★ Silver Award

31-36 Leicester Square, London
WC2H 7LH
Tel: (020) 7839 9399
Fax: (020) 7930 8122
E-mail: reshamp@radisson.com
➤ LEICESTER SQUARE
Country-house-style hotel in the
heart of theatreland. Within walking
distance of the main shopping areas
and tourist attractions.
Bedrooms: 98 double, 10 twin,
16 triple
Bathrooms: 124 en suite
Bed & Breakfast: single £179.00-
£289.00, double £199.00-£309.00
Evening meal: 1800 (l.o. 2300)
Methods of payment: Mastercard/
Visa/Barclaycard/American Express/
JCB/Eurocard/Diners/Switch/
Eurocheque

Radisson Edwardian Kenilworth

Great Russell Street, London
WC1B 3LB
Tel: (020) 7637 3477
Fax: (020) 7631 3133
➤ TOTTENHAM COURT ROAD
Thoroughly English hotel near to
theatreland, Oxford Street shops
and the City.
Bedrooms: 54 single, 82 double,
42 twin, 7 triple

hotels & b&bs

Bathrooms: 185 en suite
Evening meal: 1800 (l.o. 2200)
Methods of payment: Mastercard/
Visa/Barclaycard/American Express/
JCB/Eurocard/Diners/Switch/Delta/
Eurocheque
❏ ✿ ☎ ▯ ◉ ⊟ 🚗 ♟

Radisson Edwardian Marlborough

Bloomsbury Street, London
WC1B 3QD
Tel: (020) 7636 5601
Fax: (020) 7636 0532
↔ **TOTTENHAM COURT ROAD**
Close to the British Museum and in
the heart of Bloomsbury, London's
literary centre. Internet access
available from all rooms at an extra
cost.
Bedrooms: 15 single, 99 double,
56 twin
Bathrooms: 170 en suite
Evening meal: 1750 (l.o. 2200)
Methods of payment: Mastercard/
Visa/Barclaycard/American Express/
JCB/Eurocard/Diners/Switch/Delta/
Eurocheque
❏ ✿ ☎ ◉ ⊟ ♟

Radisson Edwardian Mountbatten

20 Monmouth Street, Seven Dials,
Covent Garden, London WC2H 9HD
Tel: (020) 7836 4300
Fax: (020) 7240 3540
E-mail: resmoun@radisson.com
↔ **COVENT GARDEN**
Delightful English country-house-
style hotel, including memorabilia
from Lord Mountbatten's family
home. Convenient for the West End
and theatreland.
Bedrooms: 19 single, 81 double,
20 twin
Bathrooms: 120 en suite
Bed & Breakfast: single £139.00-
£199.00, double £199.00-£229.00
Evening meal: 1800 (l.o. 2300)
Methods of payment: Mastercard/
Visa/Barclaycard/American Express/
JCB/Eurocard/Diners/Switch/Delta/
Eurocheque
❏ ✿ ☎ ✍ ▯ ◉ ♟

Radisson Edwardian Pastoria Hotel

3-6 St Martin's Street, Leicester
Square, London WC2H 7HL

Tel: (020) 7930 8641
Fax: (020) 7925 0551
↔ **LEICESTER SQUARE**
The hotel is located at the centre of
many top attractions, including the
West End and theatreland. The hotel
is decorated in a charming
Edwardian style.
Bedrooms: 10 single, 18 double,
30 twin
Bathrooms: 58 en suite
Evening meal: 1200 (l.o. 2200)
Methods of payment: Mastercard/
Visa/Barclaycard/American Express/
JCB/Eurocard/Diners/Switch/Delta/
Eurocheque
❏ ✿ ☎ ✍ ▯ ◉ ⊟ ♟

Renaissance London Chancery Court Hotel

252 High Holborn, London
WC1V 7EN
Tel: (020) 7829 9888
Fax: (020) 7829 9889
E-mail: sales.chancerycourt@
renaissancehotels.com
↔ **HOLBORN**
Stunning new luxury hotel in
landmark 1914 building near Covent
Garden, the British Museum,
Theatreland and the City of London.
Bedrooms: 272 single, 272 double,
71 twin
Bathrooms: 357 en suite
Bed & Breakfast: single £290.00-
£325.00, double £290.00-£325.00
Evening meal: 1830 (l.o. 2300)
Methods of payment: Mastercard/
Visa/Barclaycard/American Express/
JCB/Eurocard/Diners/Switch/Delta/
Visa Electron
❏ ✿ ☎ ✍ ▯ ◉ ⊟ 🚗 ♟

Royal Adelphi Hotel ◆◆

21 Villiers Street, London WC2N 6ND
Tel: (020) 7930 8764
Fax: (020) 7930 8735
E-mail: info@royaladelphi.co.uk
↔/⇌ **CHARING CROSS,**
↔ **EMBANKMENT**
Two minutes from Trafalgar Square
and Covent Garden and close to
theatreland.
Bedrooms: 20 single, 12 double,
13 twin, 2 triple
Bathrooms: 34 en suite, 4 shared
Bed & Breakfast: single £50.00-
£70.00, double £70.00-£90.00
Evening meal: 1800 (l.o. 2300)

Methods of payment: Mastercard/
Visa/Barclaycard/American Express
Eurocard/Diners/Switch/Delta
❏ ✿ ☎ ◉ ⊟ 🚗 ♟

St Athans Hotel ◆

20 Tavistock Place, Russell Square,
London WC1H 9RE
Tel: (020) 7837 9140/
(020) 7837 9627
Fax: (020) 7833 8352
↔ **RUSSELL SQUARE**
Small, family-run hotel.
Bedrooms: 14 single, 13 double,
15 twin, 1 triple, 5 family
Bathrooms: 8 en suite, 15 shared
Bed & Breakfast: single £30.00-
£40.00, double £40.00-£50.00
Methods of payment: Mastercard/
Visa/Barclaycard/American Express
JCB/Eurocard/Diners/Eurocheque
▥ ◉ ⊟ ♟

St Giles Hotel

Bedford Avenue, London WC1B 3AS
Tel: (020) 7300 3000/
(020) 7300 3050
Fax: (020) 7300 3003
E-mail: vhaynes@stgiles.com
↔ **TOTTENHAM COURT ROAD**
Situated at the junction of Oxford
Street and Tottenham Court Road.
Close to the British Museum.
Underground car park (NCP).
Bedrooms: 124 single, 310 double,
219 twin, 13 triple
Bathrooms: 666 en suite
Bed & Breakfast: single £104.95-
£108.95, double £145.90-£151.90
Evening meal: 1700 (l.o. 2230)
Parking for: 140
Methods of payment: Mastercard/
Visa/Barclaycard/American Express/
Eurocard/Diners/Switch/Delta
❏ ✿ ☎ ▯ ◉ ⊟ ♟ 🚗 ▦

The Savoy

★ ★ ★ ★ ★ Gold Award
The Strand, London WC2R 0EU
Tel: (020) 7836 4343
Fax: (020) 7240 6040
E-mail: info@the-savoy.co.uk
↔/⇌ **CHARING CROSS**
Midway between the City and the
West End, in the heart of theatreland,
and with excellent views of the Thames.
Bedrooms: 55 single, 100 twin,
52 family
Bathrooms: 207 en suite

hotels & b&bs

Bed & Breakfast: single £245.00-£445.40, double £295.00-£481.60
Evening meal: 1800 (l.o. 2315)
Parking for: 58
Methods of payment: Mastercard/Visa/Barclaycard/American Express/JCB/Eurocard/Diners/Switch/Delta/Eurocheque
❑ 📞 ✏ 🔲 ◑ 🛏 🍴 🚗 🔲

Swissotel, London – The Howard ★★★★★ Silver Award

Temple Place, London WC2R 2PR
Tel: (020) 7836 3555
Fax: (020) 7379 4547
E-mail: reservations@thehoward london.com
✈ **TEMPLE**
Overlooking the Thames at Victoria Embankment, close to Covent Garden and the City. Elegant boutique hotel with warm personalised service.
Bedrooms: 61 double, 49 twin, 4 triple, 21 family
Bathrooms: 135 en suite
Bed only: single £310.00, double £310.00
Evening meal: 1830 (l.o. 2300)
Parking for: 30
Methods of payment: Mastercard/Visa/Barclaycard/American Express/JCB/Eurocard/Diners/Switch/Delta/Eurocheque
❑ 📞 ✏ 🔲 ◑ 🛏 🍴 🚗

Thistle Bloomsbury

Bloomsbury Way, London WC1A 2SD
Tel: (020) 7242 5881
Fax: (020) 7831 0225
E-mail: bloomsbury@thistle.co.uk
✈ **HOLBORN**
Edwardian hotel built in 1898 with traditional-style décor. Kingsley II bar brasserie and full conference facilities.
Bedrooms: 8 single, 32 double, 79 twin, 14 triple, 5 family
Bathrooms: 138 en suite
Bed & Breakfast: single £174.95-£198.95, double £211.90-£240.90
Evening meal: 1730 (l.o. 2200)
Methods of payment: Mastercard/Visa/Barclaycard/American Express/JCB/Eurocard/Diners/Switch/Delta/Eurocheque
❑ 🌀 📞 ✏ 🔲 ◑ 🛏 🍴

Thistle Charing Cross

Strand, London WC2N 5HX
Tel: (020) 7839 7282
Fax: (020) 7747 8454
E-mail: charingx@thistle.co.uk
✈/🚇 **CHARING CROSS**
In the heart of London, close to theatreland and the art galleries, with easy access to airports, trains and buses. Grade II Listed building.
Bedrooms: 200 twin, 38 triple
Bathrooms: 238 en suite
Bed & Breakfast: double £230.00-£275.00
Methods of payment: Mastercard/Visa/Barclaycard/American Express/Diners/Switch/Delta/Eurocheque
❑ 🌀 📞 ✏ 🔲 ◑ 🛏 🍴

Thistle Kings Cross

100 King's Cross Road, London WC1X 9DT
Tel: (020) 7278 2434
Fax: (020) 7833 0798
✈/🚇 **KING'S CROSS**
Centrally located hotel, a few minutes' walk from King's Cross station and Thameslink.
Bedrooms: 29 single, 32 double, 261 twin, 29 triple
Bathrooms: 351 en suite
Bed & Breakfast: single £126.50-£154.50, double £145.00-£173.00
Evening meal: 1800 (l.o. 2145)
Parking for: 35
Methods of payment: Mastercard/Visa/Barclaycard/American Express/Diners/Switch/Delta
❑ 🌀 📞 ✏ 🔲 ◑ 🍴 🚗

Thistle Trafalgar Square

Whitcomb Street, London WC2H 7HG
Tel: (020) 7930 4477
Fax: (020) 7925 2149
E-mail: trafalgar.square@thistle.co.uk
✈/🚇 **CHARING CROSS**
Located between Trafalgar Square and Leicester Square, ideal for theatreland, shopping, sightseeing and business.
Bedrooms: 36 single, 40 double, 56 twin
Bathrooms: 132 en suite
Bed & Breakfast: single £169.95-£224.95, double £214.90-£239.90
Evening meal: 1700 (l.o. 2300)

Methods of payment: Mastercard/Visa/Barclaycard/American Express/JCB/Diners/Switch/Delta
❑ 🌀 📞 ✏ 🔲 ◑ 🛏 🍴

W2
Paddington/Bayswater

Abbey Court & Westpoint Hotel ◆◆

170-174 Sussex Gardens, London W2 1TP
Tel: (020) 7402 0281/ (020) 7402 0704
Fax: (020) 7224 9114
E-mail: info@abbeycourt.com
✈ **PADDINGTON,**
✈ **LANCASTER GATE**
Good value accommodation in central London, with easy access to London's tourist attractions and shopping areas. Within walking distance of Hyde Park. Car parking available.
Bedrooms: 26 single, 39 double, 23 twin, 24 triple, 8 family
Bathrooms: 88 en suite, 9 shower only, 10 shared
Bed & Breakfast: single £46.00-£52.00, double £64.00-£74.00
Parking for: 35
Methods of payment: Mastercard/Visa/Barclaycard/American Express/Eurocard/Switch/Delta/Eurocheque
❑ 📞 🔲 Ⓜ ◑ 🛏 ♿ 🚗

Admiral Hotel ◆◆

143 Sussex Gardens, Hyde Park, London W2 2RY
Tel: (020) 7723 7309
Fax: (020) 7723 8731
E-mail: frank@admiral143.demon. co.uk
✈/🚇 **PADDINGTON,**
✈ **LANCASTER GATE**
A bed and breakfast with 19 en suite bedrooms, five minutes from Hyde Park and Paddington station. Clean and comfortable accommodation at economic prices.
Bedrooms: 2 single, 2 double, 6 twin, 4 triple, 5 family
Bathrooms: 19 en suite, 1 shared
Bed & Breakfast: single £52.00-£55.00, double £65.00-£80.00
Parking for: 1

hotels & b&bs

Gower Hotel ◆◆

129 Sussex Gardens, Hyde Park,
London W2 2RX
Tel: (020) 7262 2262
Fax: (020) 7262 2006
E-mail: gower@stavrouhotels.co.uk
⊖/⇄ **PADDINGTON**
Family-run hotel, close to
Paddington station, Hyde Park,
Madame Tussaud's and Oxford
Street. Victorian Grade II Listed
building.
Bedrooms: 5 single, 3 double, 2 twin,
8 triple, 2 family
Bathrooms: 18 en suite, 1 shared
Bed & Breakfast: single £35.00-
£58.00, double £45.00-£76.00
Parking for: 1
Methods of payment: Mastercard/
Visa/Barclaycard/American Express/
Eurocard/Diners/Switch/Delta/
Eurocheque
▢✿⌕▥◑⇋🖨🚗

Grosvenor Court Hotel

27 Devonshire Terrace, London
W2 3PD
Tel: (020) 7262 2204
Fax: (020) 7402 9351
E-mail: info@grosvenor-court.co.uk
⊖/⇄ **PADDINGTON**
Bedrooms: 15 single, 62 double,
44 twin, 31 triple, 5 family
Bathrooms: 157 en suite
Bed and breakfast: single £100.00,
double £125.00
Evening meal: 1800 (l.o. 2200)
Methods of payment: Mastercard/
Visa/Barclaycard/American Express/
Diners/Switch/Delta/
▢✿⌕🖂◑⇋

Hilton London Hyde Park

129 Bayswater Road, Hyde Park,
London W2 4RJ
Tel: (020) 7221 2217
Fax: (020) 7229 0557
E-mail: reservations@hydepark.
stakis.co.uk
⊖ **QUEENSWAY/BAYSWATER**
Traditional British hotel offering a
warm welcome to both business
and holiday travellers.
Bedrooms: 25 single, 52 double,
51 twin, 1 triple
Bathrooms: 126 en suite
Bed only: single £155.00-£185.00,
double £175.00-£195.00

Evening meal: 1900 (l.o. 2200)
Methods of payment: Mastercard/
Visa/Barclaycard/American Express/
Eurocard/Diners/Switch/Eurocheque
▢✿⌕✆⌕🖂◑⇋🍴

Hyde Park House ◆

48 St Petersburgh Place,
Queensway, London W2 4LD
Tel: (020) 7229 9652/
(020) 7229 1687
⊖ **BAYSWATER/QUEENSWAY**
Near Hyde Park and Queensway and
convenient for restaurants and wine
bars.
Bedrooms: 4 single, 3 double, 2 twin,
3 triple
Bathrooms: 1 private, 4 shared
Bed & Breakfast: single £30.00,
double £40.00
▢✿▥⇋

Hyde Park Rooms Hotel ◆

137 Sussex Gardens, Hyde Park,
London W2 2RX
Tel: (020) 7723 0225/
(020) 7723 0965
⊖/⇄ **PADDINGTON**
Small, family-run, centrally located
hotel. Within walking distance of
Hyde Park and Paddington station.
Car parking available.
Bedrooms: 5 single, 6 double,
2 twin, 2 triple, 1 family
Bathrooms: 6 en suite, 2 shared
Bed & Breakfast: single £30.00-
£40.00, double £40.00-£45.00
Parking for: 1
Methods of payment: Mastercard/
Visa/Barclaycard/American Express/
Diners/Eurocheque
▢▥◑⇋🚗

Hyde Park Ryan Hotel

66 Lancaster Gate, Bayswater Road,
London W2 3NZ
Tel: (020) 7262 5090
Fax: (020) 7723 1244
E-mail: hotel@hydepark-ryan.com
⊖ **LANCASTER GATE**
Set in a Georgian terrace and close
to Kensington Gardens, the Hyde
Park Ryan is convenient for theatres
and museums.
Bedrooms: 13 single, 62 double,
100 twin, 7 triple, 3 family
Bathrooms: 182 en suite
Evening meal: 1800 (l.o. 2145)

Methods of payment: Mastercard/
Visa/Barclaycard/American Express/
Diners/Switch/Delta/Eurocheque
▢✿⌕✆⌕🖂◑⇋🚗🍴

Jarvis International Hyde Park

150 Bayswater Road, London
W2 4RT
Tel: (020) 7229 1212
Fax: (020) 7229 2623
E-mail: jihydepark@jarvis.co.uk
⊖ **QUEENSWAY/NOTTING HILL**
Overlooking Kensington Palace
Gardens, a few minutes from Oxford
Street and the West End.
Bedrooms: 37 single, 71 double,
105 twin
Bathrooms: 213 en suite
Bed & Breakfast: single £60.00-
£150.00, double £120.00-£175.00
Evening meal: 1730 (l.o. 2215)
Parking for: 34
Methods of payment: Mastercard/
Visa/Barclaycard/American Express/
JCB/Eurocard/Diners/Switch/Delta/
Eurocheque
▢✿⌕✆🖂◑⇋🚗🍴🚗

Kingsway Hotel ◆◆

27 Norfolk Square, Hyde Park,
London W2 1RX
Tel: (020) 7723 5569/
(020) 7723 7784
Fax: (020) 7723 7317
E-mail: kingsway.hotel@btinternet.
com
⊖/⇄ **PADDINGTON**
Owner-managed hotel situated in a
quiet garden square close to Hyde
Park and Paddington station.
Bedrooms: 9 single, 7 double,
7 twin, 3 triple, 3 family
Bathrooms: 29 en suite, 2 shared
Bed & Breakfast: single £42.00-
£62.00, double £56.00-£82.00
Methods of payment: Mastercard/
Visa/American Express/JCB/
Eurocard/Diners/Switch/Delta/
Eurocheque
▢✿⌕▥◑✗🖂◑⇋🚗

Lancaster Court Hotel ◆◆

202-204 Sussex Gardens, Hyde
Park, London W2 3UA
Tel: (020) 7402 8438/
(020) 7402 6369
Fax: (020) 7706 3794

hotels & b&bs

E-mail: lch300999@compuserve.com

PADDINGTON, LANCASTER GATE

Centrally located. Close to tourist attractions. Two minutes' walk from Hyde Park. Near A2 Airbus stop, Lancaster Gate and Paddington stations. Conference facilities. Luggage room. Parking facilities available at £12 per car per day.
Bedrooms: 13 single, 10 double, 7 twin, 7 triple, 5 family
Bathrooms: 24 en suite, 14 shower only, 2 shared
Bed only: single £32.00–£68.00, double £48.00–£85.00
Parking for: 10
Methods of payment: Mastercard/Visa/Barclaycard/American Express/JCB/Eurocard/Diners/Switch/Delta/Eurocheque

London Guards Hotel ◆◆◆

36-37 Lancaster Gate, London W2 3NA
Tel: (020) 7402 1101
Fax: (020) 7262 2551
E-mail: info@londonguardshotel.co.uk

LANCASTER GATE

All rooms are en suite with security boxes and fridges; daily servicing. Reception open 24 hours. Coffee shop and bar.
Bedrooms: 2 single, 14 double, 11 twin, 9 triple, 4 family
Bathrooms: 40 en suite
Bed & Breakfast: single £90.00–£100.00, double £100.00–£110.00
Evening meal: 1900 (l.o. 2100)
Methods of payment: Mastercard/Visa/Barclaycard/American Express/Eurocard/Diners/Switch/Delta

Manor Court Hotel ◆

7 Clanricarde Gardens, London W2 4JJ
Tel: (020) 7727 5407/
(020) 7792 3361
Fax: (020) 7229 2875

NOTTING HILL GATE

Bed and breakfast hotel run by management.
Bedrooms: 5 single, 5 double, 4 twin, 5 triple, 1 family
Bathrooms: 6 en suite, 3 private, 7 shower only, 4 shared

Bed & Breakfast: single £35.00–£50.00, double £50.00–£65.00
Methods of payment: Mastercard/Visa/American Express/JCB/Eurocard/Diners/Switch/Delta/Eurocheque

Mitre House Hotel ◆◆◆

178-184 Sussex Gardens, Hyde Park, London W2 1TU
Tel: (020) 7723 8040/
(020) 7402 5695
Fax: (020) 7402 0990
E-mail: reservations@mitrehouse hotel.com

PADDINGTON

A family-run hotel with en suite facilities. Convenient for shops and sights. Free parking. Junior and family suites available.
Bedrooms: 9 single, 18 double, 26 twin, 17 triple
Bathrooms: 70 en suite, 3 shared
Bed & Breakfast: single £60.00–£70.00, double £80.00
Parking for: 20
Methods of payment: Mastercard/Visa/Barclaycard/American Express/JCB/Eurocard/Diners/Eurocheque

Mornington Hotel

12 Lancaster Gate, London W2 3LG
Tel: (020) 7262 7361
Fax: (020) 7706 1028
E-mail: peter.elmquist@mornington.co.uk

LANCASTER GATE

Hotel situated in a quiet residential street opposite Hyde Park. Victorian exterior with cosy and comfortable interior.
Bedrooms: 22 single, 14 double, 19 twin, 2 triple, 9 family
Bathrooms: 66 en suite
Bed & Breakfast: single £110.00–£135.00, double £125.00–£155.00
Methods of payment: Mastercard/Visa/Barclaycard/American Express/JCB/Eurocard/Diners/Switch/Delta/Eurocheque

Nayland Hotel ◆◆◆

132-134 Sussex Gardens, London W2 1UB
Tel: (020) 7723 4615
Fax: (020) 7402 3292
E-mail: naylandhotel@easynet.co.uk

PADDINGTON, LANCASTER GATE

Close to Paddington and Lancaster Gate stations. Madame Tussaud's and Buckingham Palace very near. Walking distance to Hyde Park and Oxford Street.
Bedrooms: 11 single, 8 double, 17 twin, 5 triple
Bathrooms: 41 en suite
Bed & Breakfast: single £55.00–£63.00, double £65.00–£84.00
Parking for: 5
Methods of payment: Mastercard/Visa/Barclaycard/American Express/JCB/Eurocard/Diners/Switch/Delta/Eurocheque

The New Linden Hotel

58-60 Leinster Square, London W2 4PS
Tel: (020) 7221 4321
Fax: (020) 7727 3156
E-mail: newlindenhotel@vienna-group.co.uk

BAYSWATER

Small, friendly and comfortable hotel situated in the heart of Bayswater.
Bedrooms: 5 single, 10 double, 34 twin, 3 triple
Bathrooms: 52 en suite
Bed & Breakfast: single £90.00–£100.00, double £110.00–£120.00
Methods of payment: Mastercard/Visa/Barclaycard/American Express/Eurocard/Diners/Switch/Delta

Norfolk Plaza Hotel

29-33 Norfolk Square, London W2 1RX
Tel: (020) 7723 0792
Fax: (020) 7224 8770
E-mail: reservations@norfolkplaza hotel.co.uk

PADDINGTON

Edwardian Grade II Listed building located in a quiet garden square. One minute's walk from Paddington station and Heathrow Express.
Bedrooms: 1 single, 8 double, 50 twin, 22 triple, 6 family
Bathrooms: 87 en suite
Bed & Breakfast: single £71.00–£100.00, double £88.00–£125.00
Methods of payment: Mastercard/Visa/Barclaycard/American Express/JCB/Eurocard/Diners

The Bed & Breakfast and Homestay Association

ooking for Accommodation in a Private London Home?

ntact a BBHA agency and you can be sure of finding accommodation that has reached high andards, both in quality and warmth of welcome, as well as offering good value for money.

e BBHA was formed in 1998 to maintain and improve standards of Bed & Breakfast commodation in London homes. BBHA homes are regularly inspected by agency owners ho, between them, have over 100 years experience in the Bed & Breakfast industry.

ontact individual BBHA members below (quoting ref: BB1):

Home in London
Black Lion Lane
ndon W6 9BE

´: +44(0)20 8748 1943
x: +44(0)20 8747 2701

nail: info@athomeinlondon.co.uk
RL: www.athomeinlondon.co.uk

ntact: Maggie Dobson
~~~

Uptown Reservations
41 Paradise Walk
London SW3 4JL

Tel: +44(0)20 7351 3445
Fax: +44(0)20 7351 9383

Email: inquiries@uptownres.co.uk
URL: www.uptownres.co.uk

Contact: Monica Barrington
~~~

st & Guest Services
3 Dawes Road
ndon SW6 7DU

l: +44(0)20 7385 9922
x: +44(0)20 7386 7575

nail: acc@host-guest.co.uk
RL: www.host-guest.co.uk

ntact: Carol Rutter
~~~

Welcome Assured
1 Hillcrest Avenue
Edgeware HA8 8NZ

Tel: +44(0)20 8958 3996
Fax: +44(0)20 8905 4747

Contact: Malcolm Duke
~~~

ndon Bed & Breakfast Agency Ltd
Fellows Road
ndon NW3 3JY

l: +44(0)20 7586 2768
x: +44(0)20 7586 6567

nail: stay@londonbb.com
RL: www.londonbb.com

ntact: Julia Stebbing
~~~

London Homestead Services
Coombe Wood Road
Kingston Upon Thames KT2 7JY

Tel: +44(0)20 8949 4455
Fax: +44(0)20 8549 5492

Email: lhs@netcomuk.co.uk
URL: www.lhslondon.com

Contact: Valerie Brown
~~~

Welcome Homes & Hotels
21 Kellerton Road
London SE13 5RB

Tel: +44(0)20 8265 1212
Fax: +44(0)20 8852 3243

Email: info@welcomehomes.co.uk
URL: www.welcomehomes.co.uk

Contact: Pamela Burke
~~~

Visit the BBHA Website: www.bbha.org.uk

hotels & b&bs

Norfolk Towers Hotel

34 Norfolk Place, London W2 1QW
Tel: (020) 7262 3123
Fax: (020) 7224 8687
E-mail: blake@star.u-net.com
☻/⇄ PADDINGTON
The hotel is situated close to Hyde Park and Oxford Street, with a bar and restaurant.
Bedrooms: 14 single, 22 double, 46 twin, 2 triple, 1 family
Bathrooms: 84 en suite, 1 private
Bed and breakfast: single £85.00, double £125.00
Evening meal: 1730 (l.o. 2130)
Methods of payment: Mastercard/Visa/Barclaycard/American Express/JCB/Diners/Switch/Delta
⬚ ✿ ℅ ▥ ▣ ❶ 🖴 ⬛

Olympic House Hotel ◆◆

138-140 Sussex Gardens, London W2 1UB
Tel: (020) 7723 5935
Fax: (020) 7224 8144
☻/⇄ PADDINGTON
Small, centrally located, privately run hotel.
Bedrooms: 9 single, 1 double, 11 twin, 9 triple, 6 family
Bathrooms: 30 en suite, 3 shower only, 2 shared
Bed & Breakfast: single £50.00-£55.00, double £68.00-£72.00
Parking for: 4
Methods of payment: Mastercard/Visa/Barclaycard/American Express/Switch/Eurocheque
⬚ ℅ ▥ ❶ 🖴 ⬛ ⬤

Oxford Hotel ◆◆

13-14 Craven Terrace, Paddington, London W2 3QD
Tel: (020) 7402 6860/0800 318798
Fax: (020) 7262 7574
☻/⇄ PADDINGTON
Located in a quiet one-way street, close to Hyde Park and near Lancaster Gate underground station, bus routes and the Airbus stop for Heathrow. All rooms are fitted with a microwave and fridge.
Bedrooms: 1 double, 7 twin, 9 family
Bathrooms: 17 en suite, 1 shared
Bed & Breakfast: double £65.00
Methods of payment: Mastercard/Visa/Barclaycard/American Express/Eurocard/Diners/Switch/Delta
⬚ ✿ ℅ ▥ ✂ 🖴 ⬛

Park Lodge Hotel ◆◆◆

73 Queensborough Terrace, Bayswater, London W2 3SU
Tel: (020) 7229 6424
Fax: (020) 7221 4772
E-mail: smegroup.kfc@cwcom.net
☻ BAYSWATER/QUEENSWAY
Situated in Bayswater.
Bedrooms: 11 single, 10 double, 5 twin, 2 triple, 1 family
Bathrooms: 29 en suite
Bed & Breakfast: single £60.00-£75.00
Methods of payment: Mastercard/Visa/Barclaycard/American Express/Diners/Switch/Delta/Eurocheque
⬚ ✿ ℅ ▥ ❶ ⬛

Parkwood Hotel ◆◆

4 Stanhope Place, London W2 2HB
Tel: (020) 7402 2241
Fax: (020) 7402 1574
E-mail: pkwdhotel@aol.com
☻ MARBLE ARCH
Small townhouse hotel with friendly atmosphere in a quiet area close to Marble Arch and Hyde Park.
Bedrooms: 3 single, 2 double, 6 twin, 3 triple
Bathrooms: 12 en suite, 2 shared
Bed & Breakfast: single £48.00-£74.50, double £92.50
Methods of payment: Mastercard/Visa/Barclaycard/Eurocard/Switch/Delta/Eurocheque
⬚ ✿ ℅ ▥ ❶ 🖴 ⬛

The Pavilion Holiday Villa Hotel

37 Leinster Gardens, London W2 3AR
Tel: (020) 7258 0269
Fax: (020) 7723 7295
E-mail: holiday.villa@virgin.net
☻ BAYSWATER,
☻/⇄ PADDINGTON
Friendly hotel situated within easy walking distance of Hyde Park and the West End. With six conference rooms.
Bedrooms: 15 single, 32 double, 41 twin, 9 triple
Bathrooms: 97 en suite
Bed & Breakfast: single £65.00-£95.00, double £88.00-£130.00
Evening meal: 1800 (l.o. 2130)
Methods of payment: Mastercard/Visa/American Express/JCB/Diners/Switch/Delta
⬚ ✿ ℅ ▥ ❶ 🖴 ⬛ ▦

Plaza on Hyde Park

Lancaster Gate, London W2 3LG
Tel: (020) 7262 5022
Fax: (020) 7724 8666
E-mail: sales.plazaonhydepark@corushotels.com
☻ LANCASTER GATE
The hotel is opposite Hyde Park and close to Marble Arch and Oxford Street.
Bedrooms: 98 single, 148 double, 156 twin
Bathrooms: 402 en suite
Bed only: single £115.50-£315.00, double £136.50-£315.00
Evening meal: 1730 (l.o. 2300)
Methods of payment: Mastercard/Visa/Barclaycard/American Express/JCB/Eurocard/Diners/Switch/Delta/Eurocheque
⬚ ✿ ℅ ✂ ▣ ❶ 🖴 ⬛ ⬤

Rhodes House Hotel ◆◆◆

195 Sussex Gardens, London W2 2RJ
Tel: (020) 7262 5617/(020) 7262 0537
Fax: (020) 7723 4054
E-mail: chris@rhodeshotel.com
☻/⇄ PADDINGTON,
☻ LANCASTER GATE
Family-run hotel offering a high standard of accommodation to an international clientele. Families and small groups specially catered for.
Bedrooms: 3 single, 3 double, 4 twin, 4 triple, 4 family
Bathrooms: 17 en suite
Bed & Breakfast: single £55.00-£70.00, double £70.00-£85.00
Methods of payment: Mastercard/Visa/Barclaycard/JCB/Eurocard/Switch/Eurocheque
⬚ ✿ ℅ ▥ ❶ 🖴 ⬛

Royal Lancaster Hotel ★★★★

Lancaster Terrace, London W2 2TY
Tel: (020) 7262 6737
Fax: (020) 7724 3191
E-mail: book@royallancaster.com
☻/⇄ PADDINGTON
Overlooking Hyde Park and within walking distance of Marble Arch and Oxford Street. The hotel has three conference suites, three restaurants, a lounge bar, car parking and a business centre.
Bedrooms: 3 single, 220 double, 164 twin, 7 triple, 22 family

Bathrooms: 416 en suite
Bed & Breakfast: single £273.50-£361.63, double £288.50-£391.50
Evening meal: 1830 (l.o. 2230)
Parking for: 100
Methods of payment: Mastercard/Visa/Barclaycard/American Express/JCB/Eurocard/Diners/Switch/Delta/Eurocheque

Royal Park Hotel

2-5 Westbourne Terrace, London W2 3UL
Tel: (020) 7402 6187
Fax: (020) 7224 9426
E-mail: theroyalpark@argyllhotels.com
⊖/⇌ PADDINGTON
Built in 1854, this family-run hotel is well placed for the West End.
Bedrooms: 8 single, 10 double, 35 twin, 8 triple, 2 family
Bathrooms: 63 en suite
Evening meal: 1800 (l.o. 2200)
Parking for: 15
Methods of payment: Mastercard/Visa/Barclaycard/American Express/Eurocard/Switch/Eurocheque

Royal Sussex Hotel ★★

78-84 Sussex Gardens, London W2 1UH
Tel: (020) 7723 7723
Fax: (020) 7402 6318
E-mail: info@royalsussexhotel.co.uk
⊖/⇌ PADDINGTON
Within easy reach of London's West End. All 80 bedrooms are en suite. Dining facilities are available in our restaurant/bar.
Bedrooms: 8 single, 6 double, 54 twin, 10 triple, 2 family
Bathrooms: 80 en suite
Evening meal: 1800 (l.o. 2300)
Methods of payment: Mastercard/Visa/Barclaycard/American Express/Diners/Switch/Delta/Eurocheque

St David's and Norfolk Court Hotel ◆◆

16 Norfolk Square, Hyde Park, London W2 1RS
Tel: (020) 7723 3856/ (020) 7723 4963
Fax: (020) 7402 9061
⊖/⇌ PADDINGTON

Small, friendly hotel in front of a quiet garden square.
Bedrooms: 19 single, 17 double, 10 twin, 22 triple, 6 family
Bathrooms: 37 en suite, 6 shower only, 14 shared
Bed only: single £38.00-£50.00, double £58.00-£68.00
Methods of payment: Mastercard/Visa/Barclaycard/American Express/JCB/Eurocard/Diners/Switch/Delta/Eurocheque

Sass Hotel ◆◆

10-11 Craven Terrace, London W2 3QD
Tel: (020) 7262 2325
Fax: (020) 7262 0889
E-mail: info@sasshotel.com
⊖/⇌ PADDINGTON,
⊖ LANCASTER GATE
Good-value, budget accommodation in central London. Easy access to London's tourist attractions and shopping. Walking distance to Hyde Park and underground stations. Car parking available.
Bedrooms: 8 double, 7 twin, 8 triple
Bathrooms: 23 en suite, 1 shared
Bed & Breakfast: single £25.00-£36.00, double £40.00-£50.00
Methods of payment: Mastercard/Visa/Barclaycard/American Express/Switch/Eurocheque

Springfield Hotel Applied

154 Sussex Gardens, London W2 1UD
Tel: (020) 7723 9898
Fax: (020) 7723 9898
⊖/⇌ PADDINGTON
The Springfield Hotel is situated in a quiet area giving easy access to all parts of London. Close to Hyde Park and Paddington station.
Bedrooms: 2 single, 6 double, 6 twin, 6 triple
Bathrooms: 20 en suite
Bed & Breakfast: single £35.00-£50.00, double £55.00-£65.00
Parking for: 2
Methods of payment: Mastercard/Visa/Barclaycard/American Express/JCB/Eurocard/Switch/Delta/Eurocheque

Stakis London Metropole

Edgware Road, London W2 1JU
Tel: (020) 7402 4141
Fax: (020) 7724 8866
⊖ EDGWARE ROAD
Modern hotel close to West End theatres and shops. Banqueting for up to 1,325 people.
Bedrooms: 337 double, 372 twin, 28 triple
Bathrooms: 737 en suite, 4 shared
Bed & Breakfast: single £120.00-£210.00, double £120.00-£210.00
Evening meal: 1800 (l.o. 2300)
Methods of payment: Mastercard/Visa/Barclaycard/American Express/JCB/Eurocard/Diners/Switch/Delta/Eurocheque

Thistle Hyde Park

90-92 Lancaster Gate, London W2 3NR
Tel: (020) 7262 2711
Fax: (020) 7262 2147
⊖/⇌ PADDINGTON
A haven of traditional comfort, facing Hyde Park. Easy access to the City, West End and Heathrow.
Bedrooms: 10 single, 28 double, 16 twin
Bathrooms: 54 en suite
Evening meal: 1830 (l.o. 2230)
Parking for: 25
Methods of payment: Mastercard/Visa/Barclaycard/American Express/Eurocard/Diners/Switch/Delta/Eurocheque

Thistle Kensington Gardens

104 Bayswater Road, London W2 3HL
Tel: (020) 7262 4461
Fax: (020) 7706 4560
⊖/⇌ PADDINGTON,
⊖ BAYSWATER
Modern hotel overlooking Kensington Gardens and Hyde Park. Close to shops and tourist attractions. Car parking available, at a small fee.
Bedrooms: 48 single, 81 double, 41 twin, 5 triple
Bathrooms: 175 en suite
Bed & Breakfast: single £152.50-£172.50, double £185.00-£205.00
Evening meal: 1800 (l.o. 2215)

hotels & b&bs

Parking for: 80
Methods of payment: Mastercard/Visa/Barclaycard/American Express/Diners/Switch/Eurocheque

Thistle Lancaster Gate

75-89 Lancaster Gate, London W2 3NN
Tel: (020) 7402 4272
Fax: (020) 7706 4156
E-mail: lancaster.gate@thistle.co.uk
⊖/⇄ PADDINGTON,
⊖LANCASTER GATE
Opposite Kensington Gardens and Hyde Park. Within easy reach of Oxford Street and the West End.
Bedrooms: 76 single, 74 double, 209 twin, 26 triple, 5 family
Bathrooms: 390 en suite
Bed only: single £125.00–£145.00, double £145.00–£170.00
Evening meal: 1700 (l.o. 2300)
Methods of payment: Mastercard/Visa/Barclaycard/American Express/JCB/Diners/Switch/Delta/Eurocheque

Wedgewood Hotel

49-51 Leinster Square, London W2 4PU
Tel: (020) 7229 8990/(020) 7792 3536
Fax: (020) 7792 8927
E-mail: wedgewood@btinternet.com
⊖ BAYSWATER
Set in the heart of Bayswater, the Wedgewood Hotel welcomes visitors to London with its own special blend of elegance and comfort.
Bedrooms: 6 single, 13 double, 30 twin, 4 triple, 2 family
Bathrooms: 55 en suite
Bed & Breakfast: single £50.00–£55.00, double £55.00–£70.00
Evening meal: 1800 (l.o. 2100)
Methods of payment: Mastercard/Visa/Barclaycard/American Express/Eurocard/Diners

Westland Hotel ★★

154 Bayswater Road, London W2 4HP
Tel: (020) 7229 9191
Fax: (020) 7727 1054
E-mail: sisseyegh@cs.com
⊖ NOTTING HILL GATE

Small, friendly hotel, well located for West End shopping, touring or relaxing in a beautiful park.
Bedrooms: 2 single, 6 double, 19 twin, 3 triple, 1 family
Bathrooms: 31 en suite
Bed & Breakfast: single £90.00–£135.00, double £105.00–£135.00
Evening meal: 1830 (l.o. 2230)
Parking for: 9
Methods of payment: Mastercard/Visa/Barclaycard/American Express/JCB/Eurocard/Diners/Switch/Delta/Eurocheque

Westminster Hotel

16 Leinster Square, London W2 4PR
Tel: (020) 7221 9131
Fax: (020) 7221 4073
E-mail: westminsterhotel@vienna-group.co.uk
⊖ BAYSWATER,
⊖/⇄ PADDINGTON
Victorian hotel. Central London location close to Hyde Park. Convenient for major shopping areas, museums and places of interest.
Bedrooms: 30 single, 27 double, 51 twin, 8 triple
Bathrooms: 116 en suite
Bed & Breakfast: single £105.00–£115.00, double £125.00–£145.00
Evening meal: 1800 (l.o. 2200)
Methods of payment: Mastercard/Visa/Barclaycard/American Express/Eurocard/Diners/Switch/Delta/Eurocheque

SW3/5/7
Chelsea/Earls Court/South Kensington

The Albany Hotel ◆◆◆

4-12 Barkston Gardens, London SW5 0EN
Tel: (020) 7370 6116
Fax: (020) 7244 8024
E-mail: albany@realco.co.uk
⊖ EARL'S COURT
A townhouse conversion with 79 rooms, with genuine Chinese furniture, and a subtle blend of ornate woodwork and marble.
Bedrooms: 13 single, 14 double, 42 twin, 5 triple, 5 family

Bathrooms: 79 en suite
Bed & Breakfast: single £89.00, double £109.00
Methods of payment: Mastercard/Visa/Barclaycard/American Express/Diners/Switch

The Basil Street Hotel ★★★

Basil Street, Knightsbridge, London SW3 1AH
Tel: (020) 7581 3311
Fax: (020) 7581 3693
E-mail: info@thebasil.com
⊖ KNIGHTSBRIDGE
An English country-house-style hotel in the centre of London, a short distance from Harrods.
Bedrooms: 28 single, 22 double, 21 twin, 4 triple
Bathrooms: 75 en suite, 6 shared
Bed & Breakfast: single £160.40, double £243.25
Evening meal: 1830 (l.o. 2200)
Parking for: 2
Methods of payment: Mastercard/Visa/Barclaycard/American Express/JCB/Eurocard/Diners/Switch/Delta

Beaver Hotel ◆◆◆

57-59 Philbeach Gardens, London SW5 9ED
Tel: (020) 7373 4553
Fax: (020) 7373 4555
⊖ EARL'S COURT
In a quiet, tree-lined crescent of Victorian terraced houses, close to Earl's Court Exhibition Centre, convenient for South Kensington museums and Knightsbridge shops.
Bedrooms: 17 single, 9 double, 7 twin, 5 triple
Bathrooms: 26 en suite, 3 shared
Bed & Breakfast: single £40.00–£58.00, double £85.00
Parking for: 23
Methods of payment: Mastercard/Visa/Barclaycard/American Express/Eurocard/Diners/Eurocheque

The Burns Hotel ★★★

18-26 Barkston Gardens, Kensington, London SW5 0EN
Tel: (020) 7373 3151
Fax: (020) 7370 4090
E-mail: burnshotel@vienna-group.co.uk

hotels & b&bs

↔ EARL'S COURT
Attractive Victorian building situated in a quiet residential square in Kensington, within walking distance of Earl's Court underground station.
Bedrooms: 38 single, 14 double, 43 twin, 10 triple
Bathrooms: 105 en suite
Bed & Breakfast: single £124.00, double £159.00
Evening meal: 1830 (l.o. 2130)
Methods of payment: Mastercard/Visa/Barclaycard/American Express/JCB/Diners/Switch/Delta/Eurocheque
□ ☆ ℂ ⅍ ▣ ◐ 🍴 ♨

Chelsea Green Hotel ★★★★ Townhouse

35 Ixworth Place, Chelsea, London SW3 3QX
Tel: (020) 7225 7500
Fax: (020) 7225 7555
E-mail: cghotel@dircon.co.uk
↔ SOUTH KENSINGTON
Affordably luxurious, 46-room, brand-new, air-conditioned English townhouse hotel, close to Harrods, the Kensington museums and fashionable Chelsea.
Bedrooms: 4 single, 22 double, 20 twin
Bathrooms: 46 en suite
Bed and breakfast: single £150.00, double £180.00
Evening meal: 1800 (l.o. 2200)
Methods of payment: Mastercard/Visa/Barclaycard/American Express/JCB/Eurocard/Diners/Switch/Delta
□ ℂ ⅍ ▣ ◐ 🍴 ♨ ⚑

The Cliveden Town House

26 Cadogan Gardens, London SW3 2RP
Tel: (020) 7730 6466
Fax: (020) 7730 0236
E-mail: reservations@cliveden town house.co.uk
↔ SLOANE SQUARE
Elegant 19th-century townhouse opening onto Cadogan Gardens, a quiet road two minutes from Sloane Square.
Bedrooms: 8 single, 27 double
Bathrooms: 33 en suite
Bed only: single £158.65-£188.00, double £246.75-£364.25
Methods of payment: Mastercard/Visa/Barclaycard/American Express/

Eurocard/Diners/Switch/Delta/Eurocheque
□ ℂ ⅍ ▣ ◐ 🍴 ⚑ 🌂 ♨

Comfort Inn Earl's Court ◆◆

11-13 Penywern Road, Earls Court, London SW5 9TT
Tel: (020) 7373 6514
Fax: (020) 7370 3639
E-mail: comfortinn@kenotel.co.uk
↔ EARL'S COURT
An individually owned and managed hotel. Close to Earl's Court Exhibition Centre and underground station.
Bedrooms: 13 single, 12 double, 17 twin, 11 triple
Bathrooms: 53 en suite
Bed & Breakfast: single £60.00-£65.00, double £85.00-£95.00
Methods of payment: Mastercard/Visa/Barclaycard/American Express/JCB/Diners/Switch/Delta
□ ☆ ℂ ⅍ ▣ ◐ 🍴 ⚑

Cranley Gardens Hotel

8 Cranley Gardens, London SW7 3DB
Tel: (020) 7373 3232
Fax: (020) 7373 7944
E-mail: cranleygardens@aol.com
↔ GLOUCESTER ROAD
Located in the heart of Chelsea and Kensington and close to the museums and exhibition centres.
Bedrooms: 12 single, 19 double, 41 twin, 13 triple
Bathrooms: 85 en suite
Bed & Breakfast: single £79.00-£89.00, double £99.00-£109.00
Methods of payment: Mastercard/Visa/Barclaycard/American Express/JCB/Eurocard/Diners/Switch/Delta/Eurocheque
□ ℂ ▣ ◐ 🍴 ⚑ 🌂 ♨

Eden Plaza Hotel

68-69 Queensgate, London SW7 5JJ
Tel: (020) 7370 6111
Fax: (020) 7370 0932
E-mail: eden_plaza_hotel@visit.uk.com
↔ GLOUCESTER ROAD
Centrally located in Kensington, the hotel is within easy access of the airport, London's museums, exhibition centres and the West End.

Bedrooms: 13 single, 28 double, 15 twin, 4 triple, 2 family
Bathrooms: 62 en suite
Bed & Breakfast: single £63.00-£68.00, double £73.00-£83.00
Methods of payment: Mastercard/Visa/Barclaycard/American Express/Diners
□ ☆ ℂ ⅍ ▣ ◐ 🍴

Enterprise Hotel ◆◆◆

15-25 Hogarth Road, London SW5 0QJ
Tel: (020) 7373 4502/(020) 7373 4503
Fax: (020) 7373 5115
E-mail: ehotel@aol.com
↔ EARL'S COURT
Conveniently located for the West End and Knightsbridge. Kensington High Street shops and museums are also nearby.
Bedrooms: 14 single, 19 double, 42 twin, 15 triple, 5 family
Bathrooms: 92 en suite, 3 shower only, 6 shared
Bed & Breakfast: single £49.00-£70.00, double £89.00-£99.00
Evening meal: 1800 (l.o. 2230)
Methods of payment: Mastercard/Visa/Barclaycard/American Express/JCB/Eurocard/Diners/Switch/Delta/Eurocheque
□ ℂ ▣ ◐ 🍴 ⚑

Five Sumner Place Hotel ◆◆◆◆

5 Sumner Place, South Kensington, London SW7 3EE
Tel: (020) 7584 7586
Fax: (020) 7823 9962
E-mail: reservations@sumnerplace.com
↔ SOUTH KENSINGTON
This family-owned hotel offers excellent service and personal attention. All rooms are luxuriously appointed.
Bedrooms: 3 single, 5 double, 5 twin
Bathrooms: 13 en suite, 1 shared
Bed & Breakfast: single £75.00-£99.00, double £140.00-£152.00
Methods of payment: Mastercard/Visa/Barclaycard/American Express/JCB/Eurocard/Switch/Eurocheque
□ ☆ ℂ 📺 ⅍ ▣ ◐ 🍴 ⚑

Bedrooms: 1 single, 14 double,
10 twin, 4 triple
Bathrooms: 29 en suite
Bed & Breakfast: single £73.00-
£77.00, double £92.00-£97.00
Methods of payment: Mastercard/
Visa/Barclaycard/American Express/
Eurocard/Diners/Switch/Delta/
Eurocheque

Hotel Ibis Euston

3 Cardington Street, Euston, London
NW1 2LW
Tel: (020) 7388 7777
Fax: (020) 7388 0001
E-mail: h0921@accor-hotels.com
⊖/⇌ EUSTON
Situated near Euston station.
Bedrooms: 240 double, 60 twin
Bathrooms: 300 en suite
Evening meal: 1800 (l.o. 2230)
Parking for: 100
Methods of payment: Mastercard/
Visa/Barclaycard/American Express/
Eurocard/Diners/Switch/Delta/
Eurocheque

Jarvis Marylebone

Harewood Row, Marylebone,
London NW1 6SE
Tel: (020) 7262 2707
Fax: (020) 7262 2975
⊖/⇌ MARYLEBONE
Located centrally for the West End
and City. Five minutes' walk to
Madame Tussaud's and Baker Street.
Two stops on the underground to
Paddington station and the
Heathrow Express.
Bedrooms: 22 single, 25 double,
45 twin
Bathrooms: 92 en suite
Bed & Breakfast: single £100.00-
£135.00, double £140.00-£180.00
Evening meal: 1800 (l.o. 2100)
Methods of payment: Mastercard/
Visa/Barclaycard/American Express/
Diners/Switch/Eurocheque

The Landmark London

★★★★★ Gold Award
222 Marylebone Road, London
NW1 6JQ
Tel: (020) 7631 8000
Fax: (020) 7631 8080
E-mail: reservations@thelandmark.
co.uk

⊖/⇌ MARYLEBONE
Bedrooms: 184 double, 114 twin
Bathrooms: 298 en suite
Bed only: single £316.66, double
£316.66
Evening meal: 1900 (l.o. 2230)
Parking for: 80
Methods of payment: Mastercard/
Visa/Barclaycard/American Express/
JCB/Eurocard/Diners/Switch/Delta/
Eurocheque

London Euston Travel Inn Capital

141 Euston Road, London NW1 2AU
Tel: (020) 7554 3400/
(01582) 414341
Fax: (020) 7554 3419
⊖/⇌ EUSTON
Bedrooms: 100 double, 120 twin
Bathrooms: 220 en suite
Bed & Breakfast: single £72.45,
double £78.95
Evening meal: 1700 (l.o. 2230)
Parking for: 50
Methods of payment: Mastercard/
Visa/Barclaycard/American Express/
Diners/Switch/Delta/Eurocheque

Melia White House ★★★★

Albany Street, Regent's Park, London
NW1 3UP
Tel: (020) 7387 1200
Fax: (020) 7388 0091
E-mail: melia.white.house@sdmelia.es
⊖ GREAT PORTLAND STREET
Melia White House is close to
London Zoo and Madame Tussaud's
and about ten minutes' walk from
Oxford Circus.
Bedrooms: 40 single, 294 double,
172 twin, 53 triple
Bathrooms: 559 en suite
Bed & Breakfast: single £175.00-
£222.00, double £187.00-£234.00
Evening meal: 1830 (l.o. 2230)
Parking for: 7
Methods of payment: Mastercard/
Visa/Barclaycard/American Express/
JCB/Switch/Delta/Eurocheque

Shaw Park Plaza

100-110 Euston Road, London
NW1 2AJ
Tel: (020) 7666 9000
Fax: (020) 7666 9100

E-mail: sppsales@parkplazahotels.
co.uk
⊖/⇌ KING'S CROSS/EUSTON
Modern, contemporary hotel,
situated between King's Cross and
Euston stations. All 312 rooms have
air-conditioning. Bar, restaurant,
leisure club and conference facilities.
Bedrooms: 200 double, 112 twin
Bathrooms: 312 en suite
Bed only: single £155.00-£165.00,
double £155.00-£165.00
Evening meal: 1830 (l.o. 2230)
Methods of payment: Mastercard/
Visa/Barclaycard/American Express/
JCB/Eurocard/Diners/Switch/Delta/
Eurocheque

Thistle Euston

43 Cardington Street, Euston,
London NW1 2LP
Tel: (020) 7387 4400
Fax: (020) 7387 5122
E-mail: euston@thistle.co.uk
⊖/⇌ EUSTON,
⊖ EUSTON SQUARE
Modern air-conditioned hotel with
easy access to the West End.
Weekend rates available. Adjacent
to Euston station.
Bedrooms: 60 single, 67 double,
172 twin, 44 triple, 17 family
Bathrooms: 360 en suite
Evening meal: 1730 (l.o. 2230)
Parking for: 20
Methods of payment: Mastercard/
Visa/Barclaycard/American Express/
Eurocard/Diners/Switch/Delta/
Eurocheque

SE1
Waterloo/Southwark

Days Inn Waterloo

54 Kennington Road, London SE1 7BJ
Tel: (020) 7922 1331
Fax: (020) 7922 1441
E-mail: waterloo@premierhotels.co.
uk
⊖/⇌ WATERLOO,
⊖ LAMBETH NORTH
Modern, new hotel which opened in
December 1999. Located opposite
Imperial War Museum.
Accommodation rates are per room
per night for up to a family of four,
two adults and two children, sharing.

hotels & b&bs

Bedrooms: 145 double, 17 twin
Bathrooms: 162 en suite
Bed & Breakfast: single £83.50,
double £87.50
Evening meal: 1800 (l.o. 2145)
Parking for: 25
Methods of payment: Mastercard/
Visa/Barclaycard/American Express/
Diners/Switch/Delta
❑ ✿ ☏ ⌇ ☎ ◗ ◨ ☂ 🚗

Holiday Inn Express Southwark

103-109 Southwark Street, London
SE1 0JQ
Tel: (020) 7401 2525
Fax: (020) 7401 3322
**⊖/⇌ BLACKFRIARS/
SOUTHWARK**
Bedrooms: 12 single, 31 double,
37 twin, 10 triple
Bathrooms: 90 en suite
Bed & Breakfast: single £81.00-
£95.00, double £81.00-£95.00
Parking for: 19
Methods of payment: Mastercard/
Visa/Barclaycard/American Express/
JCB/Eurocard/Diners/Switch/Delta/
Eurocheque
❑ ✿ ☏ ⌇ ☎ ◗ ◨ ☂ 🚗

London Bridge Hotel

8-18 London Bridge Street, London
SE1 9SG
Tel: (020) 7855 2200
Fax: (020) 7855 2233
E-mail: sales@london-bridge-hotel.
co.uk
⊖/⇌ LONDON BRIDGE
Privately owned hotel situated
opposite London Bridge station.
Redevelopment of an existing building
with health club, wine bar and
restaurant operated by Simply Nico.
Bedrooms: 3 single, 66 double,
50 twin
Bathrooms: 119 en suite
Bed & Breakfast: single £174.95-
£184.95, double £189.90-£199.90
Evening meal: 1800 (l.o. 2300)
Methods of payment: Mastercard/
Visa/Barclaycard/American Express/
Diners/Switch/Delta
❑ ✿ ☏ ⌇ ☎ ◗ ◨ ⏚ ☂

London County Hall Travel Inn Capital

Belvedere Road, London SE1 7PB
Tel: (020) 7902 1600
Fax: (020) 7902 1619

E-mail: ti_countyhall@whitbread.com
⊖/⇌ WATERLOO
Situated in the magnificent County
Hall, overlooking the Thames
opposite the Houses of Parliament.
Bedrooms: 213 double, 13 twin,
87 family
Bathrooms: 313 en suite
Bed only: single £62.95, double
£62.95
Evening meal: 1700 (l.o. 2215)
Methods of payment: Mastercard/
Visa/Barclaycard/American Express/
Diners/Switch/Delta/Eurocheque
❑ ✿ ☏ ☎ ◗

London Marriott Hotel, County Hall

★ ★ ★ ★ ★ Silver Award

The County Hall, London SE1 7PB
Tel: (020) 7928 5200
Fax: (020) 7928 5300
**⊖ WESTMINSTER,
⊖/⇌ WATERLOO**
High standard, 200-bedroom
property, with panoramic views
across the Thames. Featuring an
exclusive leisure club with a 25-
metre indoor pool.
Bedrooms: 138 double, 62 twin
Bathrooms: 200 en suite
Bed & Breakfast: single £198.00-
£220.00, double £198.00-£220.00
Evening meal: 1730 (l.o. 2250)
Methods of payment: Mastercard/
Visa/Barclaycard/American Express/
JCB/Eurocard/Diners/Switch/Delta/
Eurocheque
❑ ✿ ☏ ⌇ ☎ ◗ ◨ ☂ 🖾

The Mad Hatter

★ ★

3-7 Stamford Street, London SE1 9NY
Tel: (020) 7401 9222
Fax: (020) 7401 7111
E-mail: madhatter@fullers.co.uk
⊖/⇌ BLACKFRIARS
Traditional English inn offering a
high standard of accommodation
with Fuller's Ale and Pie Bar
restaurant on the ground floor.
Weekend rates available.
Bedrooms: 12 double, 18 twin
Bathrooms: 30 en suite
Bed & Breakfast: single £67.50-
£97.50, double £75.00-£105.00
Methods of payment: Mastercard/
Visa/Barclaycard/American Express/
Diners/Switch/Delta
❑ ✿ ☏ ⌇ ☎ ◗

Novotel London Waterloo

★ ★ ★

113 Lambeth Road, London SE1 7LS
Tel: (020) 7793 1010
Fax: (020) 7793 0202
E-mail: h1785@accor-hotels.com
⊖/⇌ WATERLOO
Three minutes from Waterloo station
by car. Convenient location opposite
Houses of Parliament and Big Ben.
Good transport links. Hotel has 187
new rooms all with air-conditioning
and hairdryers.
Bedrooms: 187 double
Bathrooms: 187 en suite
Bed & Breakfast: single £102.00-
£140.00, double £113.00-£172.00
Evening meal: 1900 (l.o. 2345)
Parking for: 40
Methods of payment: Mastercard/
Visa/Barclaycard/American Express/
Eurocard/Diners/Switch/Delta/
Eurocheque
❑ ✿ ☏ ⌇ ☎ ◗ ◨ ☂ 🚗

W8/9/11/14 Kensington/Notting Hill/ West Kensington/Holland Park

Avonmore Hotel

◆ ◆ ◆ ◆

66 Avonmore Road, Kensington,
London W14 8RS
Tel: (020) 7603 3121/
(020) 7603 4296
Fax: (020) 7603 4035
E-mail: avonmore.hotel@dial.pipex.
com
⊖ WEST KENSINGTON
Privately owned, with a friendly
atmosphere. Three minutes' walk
from Olympia Exhibition Centre, ten
minutes from Earl's Court Exhibition
Centre and five minutes from West
Kensington underground station.
Refurbished to a high standard.
Bedrooms: 1 single, 2 double,
3 twin, 3 triple
Bathrooms: 7 en suite, 1 shared
Bed & Breakfast: single £63.00-
£88.00, double £90.00-£100.00
Methods of payment: Mastercard/
Visa/Barclaycard/American Express/
JCB/Eurocard/Diners/Switch/Delta/
Eurocheque
❑ ✿ ☏ ◗ ◨ ⏚

Colonnade Town House Hotel

★★★ Townhouse Silver Award

2 Warrington Crescent, London
W9 1ER
Tel: (020) 7289 2167
Fax: (020) 7286 1057
E-mail: res_colonnade@etontown
ouse.com
➔ WARWICK AVENUE
A lovingly restored Victorian
mansion house in elegant Little
Venice. Luxurious townhouse with
high standard of facilities.
Bedrooms: 9 single, 20 double,
2 twin, 7 triple
Bathrooms: 48 en suite
Parking for: 8
Methods of payment: Mastercard/
Visa/Barclaycard/American Express/
JCB/Diners/Switch/Eurocheque

The Copthorne Tara

★★★★ ♿

Scarsdale Place, Kensington, London
W8 5SR
Tel: (020) 7937 7211
Fax: (020) 7937 7100
E-mail: tara.sales@mill-cop.com
➔ HIGH STREET KENSINGTON
Modern hotel near Earl's Court and
Olympia exhibition centres and with
easy access to the M4, Heathrow,
Knightsbridge and the West End. Full
meeting and business facilities
available.
Bedrooms: 365 double, 466 twin
Bathrooms: 831 en suite
Bed & Breakfast: double £196.00-
£221.00
Evening meal: 1730 (l.o. 2230)
Parking for: 86
Methods of payment: Mastercard/
Visa/Barclaycard/American Express/
JCB/Eurocard/Diners/Eurocheque

Hilton London Olympia

380 Kensington High Street, London
W14 8NL
Tel: (020) 7603 3333
Fax: (020) 7603 4846
E-mail: rom_olympia@hilton.com
➔/♿ KENSINGTON (OLYMPIA)
Convenient for Kensington High
Street and the West End. Close to
Olympia and Earls Court.

Bedrooms: 5 single, 190 double,
190 twin, 9 family
Bathrooms: 394 en suite
Bed & Breakfast: single £185.00-
£215.00, double £195.00-£225.00
Evening meal: 1700 (l.o. 2230)
Parking for: 50
Methods of payment: Mastercard/
Visa/Barclaycard/American Express/
JCB/Eurocard/Diners/Switch/Delta/
Eurocheque

Hotel Atlas-Apollo

◆◆◆

18-30 Lexham Gardens, London
W8 5JE
Tel: (020) 7835 1155/
(020) 7835 1133
Fax: (020) 7370 4853
E-mail: reservations@atlas-apollo.com
➔ EARL'S COURT
Friendly, well-established hotel
situated close to Knightsbridge,
Kensington High Street and Earl's
Court and Olympia exhibition
centres.
Bedrooms: 28 single, 7 double,
44 twin, 14 triple
Bathrooms: 93 en suite
Bed & Breakfast: single £75.00-
£85.00, double £90.00-£100.00
Methods of payment: Mastercard/
Visa/Barclaycard/American Express/
JCB/Eurocard/Switch/Delta/
Eurocheque

Kensington Guest House

◆◆

72 Holland Park Avenue, London
W11 3QZ
Tel: (020) 7229 9233
Fax: (020) 7221 1077
E-mail: hotelondon@aol.com
➔ HOLLAND PARK
Small, family-run guesthouse in a
pleasant central location. One
minute from Holland Park
underground station, buses and
Airbus direct from Heathrow. All
rooms have cable TV and cooking
facilities. English breakfast served to
bedrooms.
Bedrooms: 3 twin, 1 triple, 2 family
Bathrooms: 1 en suite, 2 shared
Methods of payment: Mastercard/
Visa/Barclaycard/American Express/
Eurocard/Diners/Switch/Delta

The Kensington

★★★★ Silver Award

Kensington House, Richmond Way,
London W14 0AX
Tel: (020) 7674 1000
Fax: (020) 7674 1050
E-mail: reservations@thekensington.
co.uk
➔ SHEPHERD'S BUSH
The Kensington is a contemporary
chic hotel, uniquely designed to
offer great value in terms of stunning
style, facilities, service and price.
Bedrooms: 16 single, 60 double,
150 twin
Bathrooms: 226 en suite
Bed & Breakfast: single £142.95-
£262.95, double £175.90-£275.90
Evening meal: 1800 (l.o. 2200)
Parking for: 28
Methods of payment: Mastercard/
Visa/Barclaycard/American Express/
JCB/Eurocard/Diners/Switch/Delta/
Eurocheque

London Kensington Hilton

★★★ Silver Award

179-199 Holland Park Avenue,
London W11 4UL
Tel: (020) 7603 3355
Fax: (020) 7602 9397
E-mail: sales_kensington@hilton.com
➔ HOLLAND PARK
Modern hotel with easy access to
exhibition centres, Holland Park and
the West End. Express bus link to
Heathrow.
Bedrooms: 19 single, 319 double,
265 twin
Bathrooms: 603 en suite
Bed & Breakfast: single £96.00-
£225.00, double £96.00-£225.00
Evening meal: 1800 (l.o. 2230)
Parking for: 100
Methods of payment: Mastercard/
Visa/Barclaycard/American Express/
Eurocard/Diners/Switch/Delta/
Eurocheque

London Lodge Hotel ★★★

134-136 Lexham Gardens, London
W8 6JE
Tel: (020) 7244 8444
Fax: (020) 7373 6661
E-mail: info@londonlodgehotel.com
➔ EARL'S COURT

hotels & b&bs

A newly refurbished townhouse hotel. All rooms are en suite with satellite TV, mini bar, hairdryer, trouser press and direct dial telephone. Close to public transport and convenient for Kensington museums and Earls Court.
Bedrooms: 7 single, 8 double, 12 twin, 1 triple
Bathrooms: 28 en suite
Bed & Breakfast: single £88.00-£135.00, double £108.00-£169.00
Evening meal: 1800 (l.o. 2230)
Methods of payment: Mastercard/Visa/American Express/JCB/Diners/Switch/Delta
⬚ ✆ ⚲ ▤ ◗ ⛟ ☂

Posthouse Kensington

Wright's Lane, London W8 5SP
Tel: 0870 400 9000
Fax: (020) 7937 8289
�subway HIGH STREET KENSINGTON
Large, modern hotel close to Kensington High Street and Kensington Gardens. Easy access to the West End.
Bedrooms: 189 single, 96 double, 259 twin, 6 triple
Bathrooms: 544 en suite, 6 shower only
Bed & Breakfast: single £130.95-£170.95, double £142.90-£182.90
Evening meal: 1730 (l.o. 2230)
Parking for: 70
Methods of payment: Mastercard/Visa/Barclaycard/American Express/JCB/Eurocard/Diners/Switch/Delta/Eurocheque
⬚ ✿ ✆ ⚲ ▤ ◗ ⛟ ☂ ⛟ ▨

Royal Garden Hotel

2-24 Kensington High Street, London W8 4PT
Tel: (020) 7937 8000
Fax: (020) 7361 1991
E-mail: guest@royalgdn.co.uk
�subway HIGH STREET KENSINGTON
Recently refurbished 400-bedroom hotel with two restaurants, health and fitness facilities, extensive conference and banqueting facilities and car parking. Excellent location overlooking Hyde Park and Kensington Gardens.
Bedrooms: 123 single, 144 double, 87 twin, 38 triple, 3 family
Bathrooms: 392 en suite, 3 private

Bed & Breakfast: single £230.00-£290.00, double £300.00-£360.00
Evening meal: 1730 (l.o. 2330)
Parking for: 160
Methods of payment: Mastercard/Visa/Barclaycard/American Express/Eurocard/Diners/Eurocheque
⬚ ✆ ⚲ ▤ ◗ ⛟ ☂ ⛟

Thistle Kensington Palace

De Vere Gardens, London W8 5AF
Tel: (020) 7937 8121
Fax: (020) 7937 2816
➘ HIGH STREET KENSINGTON
Large hotel overlooking Kensington Gardens. Close to the shopping areas of Knightsbridge and the West End.
Bedrooms: 65 single, 65 double, 140 twin, 6 triple, 22 family
Bathrooms: 298 en suite
Evening meal: 1700 (l.o. 2330)
Methods of payment: Mastercard/Visa/Barclaycard/American Express/JCB/Eurocard/Diners/Switch/Delta/Eurocheque
⬚ ✿ ✆ ⚲ ▤ ◗ ⛟ ☂

Thistle Kensington Park

16-32 De Vere Gardens, London W8 5AG
Tel: (020) 7937 8080
Fax: (020) 7937 7616
➘ HIGH STREET KENSINGTON
Located in Kensington, the hotel offers guests luxury and comfort within easy reach of the city centre.
Bedrooms: 80 single, 92 double, 134 twin, 17 triple, 30 family
Bathrooms: 353 en suite
Evening meal: 1800 (l.o. 2300)
Methods of payment: Mastercard/Visa/Barclaycard/American Express/JCB/Eurocard/Diners/Switch/Delta/Eurocheque
⬚ ✿ ✆ ⚲ ▤ ◗ ⛟ ☂

W3/4/5/6/7 Acton/Chiswick/Ealing/Hammersmith

Acton Park Hotel ★

116 The Vale, Acton, London W3 7JT
Tel: (020) 8743 9417
Fax: (020) 8743 9417
⇌ ACTON CENTRAL
Small, family-run hotel, overlooking parkland, between Heathrow and the West End. Parking available.

Bedrooms: 7 single, 4 double, 8 twin, 2 triple
Bathrooms: 21 en suite
Bed & Breakfast: single £48.00-£64.00, double £59.00-£72.00
Evening meal: 1800 (l.o. 2200)
Parking for: 15
Methods of payment: Mastercard/Visa/Barclaycard/American Express/JCB/Eurocard/Diners/Switch/Delta
⬚ ✿ ✆ ▤ ◗ ⛟ ☂ ⛟

Boston Manor Hotel ◆◆◆

146-152 Boston Road, Hanwell, London W7 2HJ
Tel: (020) 8566 1534
Fax: (020) 8567 9510
E-mail: bmh@bostonmanor.com
➘ BOSTON MANOR
Family-run hotel located close to Heathrow, with easy access to central London. Large car park and restaurant. Luxury suites available. The hotel has 24-hour reception.
Bedrooms: 10 single, 14 double, 4 twin, 2 triple, 2 family
Bathrooms: 27 en suite, 4 private, 1 shower only, 2 shared
Bed & Breakfast: single £40.00-£49.00, double £50.00-£60.00
Evening meal: 1730 (l.o. 2330)
Parking for: 20
Methods of payment: Mastercard/Visa/Barclaycard/Diners/Switch/Delta
⬚ ✿ ✆ ⚲ ◗ ⛟ ⛟

Chiswick Hotel ★★★

73 High Road, London W4 2LS
Tel: (020) 8994 1712
Fax: (020) 8742 2585
E-mail: chishot@clara.net
➘ TURNHAM GREEN
Large, carefully converted Victorian house, retaining many original features and with a friendly personal atmosphere. Located between Heathrow and central London.
Bedrooms: 28 single, 11 double, 7 twin, 4 triple, 3 family
Bathrooms: 53 en suite, 2 shared
Bed & Breakfast: single £89.25-£99.00, double £112.00-£125.00
Evening meal: 1800 (l.o. 2100)
Parking for: 20
Methods of payment: Mastercard/Visa/Barclaycard/American Express/JCB/Eurocard/Diners/Switch/Delta/Eurocheque
⬚ ✿ ✆ ◗ ⛟ ⛟ ⛟

hotels & b&bs

Creffield Lodge ◆◆

2-4 Creffield Road, Ealing, London
W5 3HN
Tel: (020) 8993 2284
Fax: (020) 8992 7082
⊖ **EALING COMMON**
Victorian-style property, located in a
quiet residential road, adjacent to
the Jarvis International Hotel. Full
use of facilities at the Jarvis
International Hotel, Ealing.
Bedrooms: 12 single, 5 double,
3 twin, 4 triple
Bathrooms: 14 en suite, 4 shared
Bed & Breakfast: single £45.00-
£75.00, double £65.00-£95.00
Evening meal: 1830 (l.o. 2230)
Parking for: 20
Methods of payment: Mastercard/
Visa/Barclaycard/American Express/
JCB/Eurocard/Diners/Switch/Delta/
Eurocheque

Foubert's Hotel ◆◆

162-166 Chiswick High Road,
London W4 1PR
Tel: (020) 8994 5202/
(020) 8995 6743
⊖ **TURNHAM GREEN**
Family-run hotel close to Heathrow
Airport and central London. Fully
licensed restaurant and cellar bars.
Live music and dancing at
weekends.
Bedrooms: 15 single, 9 double,
4 twin, 3 triple
Bathrooms: 16 en suite, 15 private,
4 shared
Bed & Breakfast: single £45.00-
£50.00, double £65.00-£70.00
Evening meal: (l.o. 2300)
Methods of payment: Mastercard/
Visa/Barclaycard/Eurocheque

Fox & Goose Hotel

Hanger Lane, London W5 1DP
Tel: (020) 8998 5864
Fax: (020) 8997 5378
E-mail: foxandgoose@fullers.co.uk
⊖ **HANGER LANE**
Built in 1997, the Fox and Goose
Hotel offers a traditional style with
modern amenities. Spacious rooms,
comfortable and inviting bar and
restaurant serving home cooked
food.

Bedrooms: 30 double, 21 twin,
3 triple
Bathrooms: 54 en suite
Evening meal: 1800 (l.o. 2130)
Methods of payment: Mastercard/
Visa/Barclaycard/American Express/
Eurocard/Diners/Switch/Delta/
Eurocheque

Hotel Orlando ◆◆

83 Shepherd's Bush Road,
Hammersmith, London W6 7LR
Tel: (020) 7603 4890
Fax: (020) 7603 4890
⊖ **HAMMERSMITH**
Bedrooms: 4 single, 1 double,
5 twin, 2 triple, 2 family
Bathrooms: 12 en suite
Bed & Breakfast: single £32.00-
£35.00, double £46.00-£52.00
Methods of payment: Mastercard/
Visa/American Express/Eurocard/
Switch/Delta/Eurocheque

Jarvis International, Ealing ★★★★

Ealing Common, London W5 3HN
Tel: (020) 8896 8400
Fax: (020) 8992 7082
⊖ **EALING COMMON**
Modern, purpose-built five-storey
building close to Ealing town centre
and within easy reach of central
London.
Bedrooms: 1 single, 133 double,
55 twin
Bathrooms: 189 en suite
Bed & Breakfast: single £146.00-
£171.00, double £177.00-£202.00
Evening meal: 1830 (l.o. 2230)
Parking for: 150
Methods of payment: Mastercard/
Visa/Barclaycard/American Express/
JCB/Eurocard/Diners/Switch/Delta/
Eurocheque

Novotel London West

1 Shortlands, Hammersmith, London
W6 8DR
Tel: (020) 8741 1555/
(020) 8237 7437
Fax: (020) 8741 2120
E-mail: h0737@accor_hotels.com
⊖ **HAMMERSMITH**
A modern, international hotel with
easy access to Heathrow and

central London; conference and
exhibition facilities and car park. All
rooms have en suite bathrooms,
satellite television and tea and
coffee facilities.
Bedrooms: 150 double, 398 twin,
77 triple
Bathrooms: 625 en suite
Bed only: single £145.00, double
£165.00
Evening meal: 1700 (l.o. 2355)
Parking for: 220
Methods of payment: Mastercard/
Visa/Barclaycard/American Express/
JCB/Eurocard/Diners/Switch/Delta/
Eurocheque

St Peters Hotel ◆◆◆

407-411 Goldhawk Road, London
W6 0SA
Tel: (020) 8741 4239
Fax: (020) 8748 3845
⊖ **STAMFORD BROOK**
A small, well-appointed
establishment where customer care
is a priority. Within easy reach of
Heathrow and central London. Good
value for money.
Bedrooms: 5 single, 5 double, 8 twin
Bathrooms: 12 en suite, 1 shared
Methods of payment: Mastercard/
Visa/Barclaycard/American Express/
Eurocard/Switch/Delta/Eurocheque

North West London

Dawson House Hotel ◆◆◆◆

72 Canfield Gardens, London
NW6 3ED
Tel: (020) 7624 0079/
(020) 7624 6525
Fax: (020) 7644 6321
E-mail: dawsonhtl@aol.com
⊖ **FINCHLEY ROAD**
Convenient for West End shops and
theatres.
Bedrooms: 6 single, 5 double, 1 twin,
2 triple, 1 family
Bathrooms: 15 en suite, 2 shared
Bed & Breakfast: single £45.00-
£50.00, double £70.00-£80.00
Methods of payment: Mastercard/
Visa/Barclaycard/American Express/
JCB/Eurocard/Diners/Switch/Delta/
Eurocheque

hotels & b&bs

Hendon Hall (A Thistle Country House Hotel) ★★★★

Ashley Lane, off Parson Street, Hendon, London NW4 1HF
Tel: (020) 8203 3341
Fax: (020) 8203 9709
E-mail: hendon.hall@thistle.co.uk
➔ HENDON CENTRAL
Elegant, 18th-century Georgian mansion set in its own grounds.
Bedrooms: 1 single, 36 double, 21 twin
Bathrooms: 58 en suite
Bed & Breakfast: single £100.00-180.00, double £110.00-£240.00
Evening meal: 1900 (l.o. 2200)
Parking for: 70
Methods of payment: Mastercard/Visa/Barclaycard/American Express/JCB/Eurocard/Diners/Switch/Delta/Eurocheque

Howard Johnson London Wembley

North Circular Road, Ealing, London NW10 7UG
Tel: (020) 8965 9200
Fax: (020) 8965 9300
E-mail: wembley@premierhotels.co.uk
➔ HANGER LANE
New hotel which opened in March 2000, offering 120 en suite bedrooms. Prices are per room, with children up to 12 years old staying free if sharing a room with parents.
Evening meal: 1800 (l.o. 2100)
Parking for: 120
Methods of payment: Mastercard/Visa/Barclaycard/American Express/Diners/Switch

Jarvis International Regent's Park Hotel

18 Lodge Road, St John's Wood, London NW8 7JT
Tel: (020) 7722 7722
Fax: (020) 7483 2408
E-mail: regentspark@jarvis.co.uk
➔ ST JOHN'S WOOD
Overlooking Lord's Cricket Ground and adjacent to Regent's Park. Close to the West End. Direct underground link to the Millennium Dome.
Bedrooms: 224 double, 149 twin, 4 family

Bathrooms: 377 en suite
Bed & Breakfast: single £210.50, double £226.00
Evening meal: 1830 (l.o. 2230)
Parking for: 80
Methods of payment: Mastercard/Visa/Barclaycard/American Express/JCB/Eurocard/Diners/Switch/Delta/Eurocheque

The Langorf Hotel & Apartments

20 Frognal, London NW3 6AG
Tel: (020) 7794 4483
Fax: (020) 7435 9055
E-mail: langorf@aol.com
➔ FINCHLEY ROAD
Elegant Edwardian residence, three minutes' walk from Finchley Road underground station. En suite bedrooms with modern comforts, 24 hour reception and room service.
Bedrooms: 1 single, 18 double, 8 twin, 4 triple
Bathrooms: 31 en suite
Bed & Breakfast: single £77.00-£82.00, double £95.00-£100.00
Methods of payment: Mastercard/Visa/Barclaycard/American Express/Eurocard/Diners/Switch/Delta/Eurocheque

Posthouse Hampstead

215 Haverstock Hill, London NW3 4RB
Tel: 0870 400 9037
Fax: (020) 7435 5586
➔ BELSIZE PARK
This modern hotel is close to Hampstead Heath and central London and is quickly reached by the nearby underground or bus.
Bedrooms: 107 single, 97 double, 103 twin, 22 triple
Bathrooms: 329 en suite
Bed & Breakfast: single £110.95-£120.95, double £122.90-£132.85
Evening meal: 1830 (l.o. 2200)
Methods of payment: Mastercard/Visa/Barclaycard/American Express/Diners/Switch/Delta

Regent's Park Marriott – London

128 King Henry's Road, Swiss Cottage, London NW3 3ST

Tel: (020) 7722 7711
Fax: (020) 7586 5822
➔ SWISS COTTAGE
Close to Regent's Park, with good access to the M1, M40 and M4 motorways.
Bedrooms: 210 double, 75 twin, 18 triple
Bathrooms: 303 en suite
Evening meal: 1800 (l.o. 2200)
Parking for: 100
Methods of payment: Mastercard/Visa/Barclaycard/American Express/JCB/Eurocard/Diners/Switch/Delta/Eurocheque

Swallow Regents Plaza Hotel

Plaza Parade, Maida Vale, London NW6 5RP
Tel: (020) 7543 6000
Fax: (020) 7543 2100
E-mail: regentsplaza@btinternet.com
➔ MAIDA VALE
Luxury hotel located ten minutes from Marble Arch, Regent's Park and Lord's Cricket Ground. The hotel has two restaurants, bar, health and leisure club, large pool, business centre, landscaped gardens and private parking.
Bedrooms: 193 double, 115 twin, 72 triple, 6 family
Bathrooms: 386 en suite
Bed & Breakfast: double £145.00-£205.00
Evening meal: 1800 (l.o. 2300)
Parking for: 141
Methods of payment: Mastercard/Visa/Barclaycard/American Express/JCB/Eurocard/Diners/Switch/Delta

North London

Costello Palace Hotel ◆◆

374 Seven Sisters Road, Finsbury Park, London N4 2PG
Tel: (020) 8802 6551
Fax: (020) 8802 9461
➔ MANOR HOUSE
Overlooking Finsbury Park, with its own car park and fully licensed bar. All rooms are en suite with facilities for making tea and coffee, Sky TV and 24-hour reception.
Bedrooms: 3 single, 17 double, 20 twin, 4 triple

hotels & b&bs

Bathrooms: 44 en suite
Bed & Breakfast: single £45.00,
double £60.00
Parking for: 35
Methods of payment: Mastercard/
Visa/Barclaycard/Switch/Delta/
Eurocheque

Europa Hotel APPLIED

60-62 Anson Road, London N7 0AA
Tel: (020) 7607 5935
Fax: (020) 7607 5909
⊖ **TUFNELL PARK**
Listed building, over 100 years old.
Bedrooms: 7 single, 6 double, 6 twin,
2 triple, 7 family
Bathrooms: 28 en suite
Bed & Breakfast: single £28.00-
£30.00, double £45.00-£50.00
Non-smoking establishment
Methods of payment: Mastercard/
Visa/Barclaycard/Eurocard/Switch/
Eurocheque

Five Kings Guest House ◆◆

59 Anson Road, Tufnell Park, London
N7 0AR
Tel: (020) 7607 3996/
(020) 7607 6466
Fax: (020) 7609 5554
⊖ **TUFNELL PARK**
Privately run guesthouse situated in a
quiet residential area. Fifteen minutes
from central London. Parking with no
restrictions available in Anson Road.
Bedrooms: 6 single, 3 double, 3 twin,
2 triple, 2 family
Bathrooms: 11 en suite, 3 shared
Bed & Breakfast: single £24.00-
£30.00, double £36.00-£44.00
Methods of payment: Mastercard/
Visa/Barclaycard/American Express/
Eurocard/Eurocheque

Hilton London Islington

53 Upper Street, London N1 0UY
Tel: (020) 7354 7700/
(020) 7354 7777
Fax: (020) 7354 7711
E-mail: revenue.manager@islington.
stakis.co.uk
⊖ **ANGEL**
Modern hotel located next to the
Business Design Centre in Islington,
with a premier Livingwell Health
Club.

Bedrooms: 3 single, 109 double,
66 twin, 6 triple
Bathrooms: 184 en suite
Bed & Breakfast: single £80.00-
£175.00, double £115.00-£230.00
Evening meal: 1800 (l.o. 2230)
Parking for: 250
Methods of payment: Mastercard/
Visa/Barclaycard/American Express/
JCB/Eurocard/Diners/Switch/Delta/
Eurocheque

Homestead ◆◆

141 Ferme Park Road, Crouch End,
London N8 9SG
Tel: (020) 8347 8768
Fax: (020) 8348 2256
⊖/≥ **FINSBURY PARK**
Victorian terraced house built in 1880.
Bedrooms: 1 double, 2 twin, 3 triple,
2 family
Bathrooms: 3 en suite, 4 private,
1 shower only
Bed & Breakfast: single £24.00-
£25.00, double £44.00-£50.00
Methods of payment: Mastercard/
Visa/Barclaycard/Eurocard/Switch/
Delta/Eurocheque

Jurys London Inn ★★★

60 Pentonville Road, Islington,
London N1 9LA
Tel: (020) 7282 5500
Fax: (020) 7282 5511
E-mail: padhraic_flavin@jurys.com
⊖/≥ **KING'S CROSS,**
⊖ **ANGEL**
City centre hotel with 229 air-
conditioned rooms accommodating
three adults or two adults and two
children at a fixed room rate.
Bedrooms: 116 double, 113 twin
Bathrooms: 229 en suite
Bed & Breakfast: single £90.00,
double £96.00
Evening meal: 1800 (l.o. 2130)
Methods of payment: Mastercard/
Visa/Barclaycard/American Express/
Eurocard/Diners/Switch/Delta/
Eurocheque

Queens Hotel ◆◆

33 Anson Road, Tufnell Park, London
N7 0RB
Tel: (020) 7607 4725
Fax: (020) 7697 9725

E-mail: queens@stavrouhotels.co.uk
⊖ **TUFNELL PARK**
Large detached Georgian property
easily accessible by underground
and buses. Shops and other
amenities nearby. Fifteen minutes to
the West End.
Bedrooms: 16 single, 10 double,
6 twin, 1 triple, 5 family
Bathrooms: 15 en suite, 7 shared
Bed & Breakfast: single £30.00-
£36.00, double £45.00-£58.00
Parking for: 3
Methods of payment: Mastercard/
Visa/Barclaycard/Eurocard/Switch/
Delta/Eurocheque

Spring Park Hotel ★

400 Seven Sisters Road, London
N4 2LX
Tel: (020) 8800 6030
Fax: (020) 8802 5652
E-mail: sphotel400@aol.com
⊖ **MANOR HOUSE,**
⊖/≥ **FINSBURY PARK**
Edwardian-style hotel overlooking
scenic Finsbury Park. Next to Manor
House underground station with
direct links to the West End and
Heathrow.
Bedrooms: 10 single, 19 double,
20 twin, 1 triple
Bathrooms: 36 en suite, 7 shared
Bed & Breakfast: single £39.00-
£55.00, double £55.00-£75.00
Evening meal: 1800 (l.o. 2300)
Parking for: 70
Methods of payment: Mastercard/
Visa/Barclaycard/American Express/
JCB/Switch/Delta/Eurocheque

White Lodge Hotel ◆◆◆

1 Church Lane, Hornsey, London
N8 7BU
Tel: (020) 8348 9765
Fax: (020) 8340 7851
≥ **HORNSEY,**
⊖ **TURNPIKE LANE**
Small, friendly family hotel offering
personal service and easy access to
all transport.
Bedrooms: 7 single, 3 double, 3 twin,
3 family
Bathrooms: 8 en suite, 3 shared
Bed & Breakfast: single £28.00-
£38.00, double £38.00-£46.00
Evening meal: 1800 (l.o. 1900)

hotels & b&bs

Methods of payment: Mastercard/Visa/Barclaycard/Eurocard/Eurocheque

□ ✿ Ⓤ ◑ ⌫ ♿

East London

Forest View Hotel ◆

227 Romford Road, Forest Gate, London E7 9HL
Tel: (020) 8534 4844
Fax: (020) 8534 8959
⇌ **FOREST GATE**
Fully equipped hotel catering for both business and tourist customers. Most rooms are en suite with tea and coffee making facilities, television, radio and telephone. Close to London Docklands.
Bedrooms: 8 single, 5 double, 2 twin, 2 triple, 3 family
Bathrooms: 3 en suite, 4 private, 3 shared
Bed & Breakfast: single £41.80, double £60.80-£72.90
Evening meal: 1830 (l.o. 2100)
Parking for: 15
Methods of payment: Mastercard/Visa/Barclaycard/JCB/Eurocard/Switch/Delta/Eurocheque

□ ✿ ⓛ ◑ ⌫ ♿ 🚗

Four Seasons Hotel Canary Wharf

46 Westferry Circus, Canary Wharf, London E14 8RS
Tel: (020) 7510 1999
Fax: (020) 7510 1998
Chic and exclusive hotel with 142 rooms including 14 suites. Four Seasons Hotel Canary Wharf combines comfort with personal service.
Bedrooms: 129 double, 13 twin
Bathrooms: 142 en suite
Evening meal: 1800 (l.o. 2330)
Parking for: 29
Methods of payment: Mastercard/Visa/Barclaycard/American Express/JCB/Eurocard/Diners/Eurocheque

□ ⓛ ✂ ◑ ♟ 🚗

Grangewood Lodge Hotel ◆

104 Clova Road, Forest Gate, London E7 9AF
Tel: (020) 8534 0637/(020) 8503 0941
Fax: (020) 8257 0392

⊖/⇌ **STRATFORD**, ⇌ **FOREST GATE**
Comfortable, budget accommodation in a quiet road, with pleasant garden. Good access to central London, Docklands and M11.
Bedrooms: 10 single, 1 double, 5 twin, 2 triple
Bathrooms: 1 shower only, 3 shared
Bed & Breakfast: single £21.00-£24.00, double £34.00-£44.00
Parking for: 2
Methods of payment: Mastercard/Visa/Barclaycard/Switch/Eurocheque

□ ✿ ⓤ ⌫ ♿ 🚗

Sleeping Beauty Motel

Travel Accommodation
543 Lea Bridge Road, Leyton, London E10 7EB
Tel: (020) 8556 8080
Fax: (020) 8556 8080
⊖/⇌ **WALTHAMSTOW CENTRAL**
Motel on four floors. New wing opened May 1998. Car and coach park.
Bedrooms: 17 double, 68 twin
Bathrooms: 85 en suite
Bed & Breakfast: single £45.00, double £50.00
Parking for: 79
Methods of payment: Mastercard/Visa/Barclaycard/American Express/JCB/Eurocard/Diners/Switch/Delta/Eurocheque

□ ✿ ⓛ 🕮 ◑ ♟ ♿ 🚗

Thistle Tower

St Katharine's Way, London E1W 1LD
Tel: (020) 7481 2575
Fax: (020) 7488 4106
E-mail: tower.businesscentre@thistle.co.uk
⇌ **FENCHURCH STREET**, ⊖ **TOWER HILL**
Next to Tower Bridge and the Tower of London and overlooking St Katharine's Dock. Close to the City and the West End. Ideally located for both business and pleasure.
Bedrooms: 89 single, 330 double, 360 twin, 22 triple
Bathrooms: 801 en suite
Bed & Breakfast: single £205.00-£245.00, double £215.00-£245.00
Evening meal: 1730 (l.o. 2230)
Parking for: 116

Methods of payment: Mastercard/Visa/Barclaycard/American Express/JCB/Eurocard/Diners/Switch/Delta/Eurocheque

□ ✿ ⓛ ✂ 🕮 ◑ ♟ ♟ 🚗

South East London

Benvenuti ◆◆◆◆

217 Court Road, Eltham, London SE9 4TG
Tel: (020) 8857 4855
Fax: (020) 8265 5635
E-mail: val.smith.benvenuti@cwcom.net
⇌ **MOTTINGHAM**
Family-run bed and breakfast. Four minutes' walk from train station. Central London is 25 minutes by train. A 15 minute direct bus ride to the Millennium Dome. Convenient for the M25, M20, A20, A2 and M2.
Bedrooms: 3 double, 1 twin, 1 triple, 1 family
Bathrooms: 2 en suite, 1 shared
Bed & Breakfast: single £30.00-£35.00, double £50.00-£60.00
Parking for: 4
Non-smoking establishment

□ ✿ ⓤ ✂ 🚗

Clarendon Hotel ★♣

8-16 Montpelier Row, Blackheath, London SE3 0RW
Tel: (020) 8318 4321
Fax: (020) 8318 4378
⇌ **BLACKHEATH**
Facing the heath and 22 minutes by train from central London. Ten minutes' walk from Greenwich, five minutes' walk from Greenwich Royal Park. Listed 250-year-old building.
Bedrooms: 40 single, 53 double, 54 twin, 32 triple, 7 family
Bathrooms: 186 en suite
Bed & Breakfast: single £65.00-£75.00, double £79.00-£95.00
Evening meal: 1830 (l.o. 2145)
Parking for: 80
Methods of payment: Mastercard/Visa/Barclaycard/American Express/JCB/Eurocard/Switch/Delta/Eurocheque

□ ✿ ⓛ ✂ 🕮 ◑ ♟ 🏨 ♟ 🚗

Holiday Inn Nelson Dock ★★★★

265 Rotherhithe Street, London SE16 5HW

apartments

Slough/Windsor Marriott Hotel

Ditton Road, Langley, Berkshire
SL3 8PT
Tel: (01753) 544244/
(020) 7591 1529
Fax: (01753) 540272
⇌ **LANGLEY**
Close to the M4 and the M25, with
easy access to London and
Heathrow. Well-appointed
bedrooms, restaurant and leisure
club.
Bedrooms: 261 double, 119 twin
Bathrooms: 380 en suite
Bed & Breakfast: double £145.00-
£195.00
Evening meal: 1830 (l.o. 2200)
Parking for: 600
Methods of payment: Mastercard/
Visa/Barclaycard/American Express/
Eurocard/Diners/Switch/Delta/
Eurocheque
🖵🌣📞🏌🗂🛏🍴♨🛁🐾

South Lodge Hotel

Brighton Road, Lower Beeding, West
Sussex RH13 6PS
Tel: (01403) 891711
Fax: (01403) 891766
E-mail: enquiries@southlodgehotel.
co.uk
⇌ **HORSHAM**
A 41 bedroom AA 4 Red Star
Victorian country house set in 93
acres, overlooking the South Downs.
Ideal for leisure or business. Golf at
nearby Mannings Heath.
Bedrooms: 1 single, 39 double,
1 twin
Bathrooms: 41 en suite
Bed & Breakfast: single £173.95-
£373.95 double £212.90-£387.90
Evening meal: 1930 (l.o. 2200)
Parking for: 100
Methods of payment: Mastercard/
Visa/Barclaycard/American Express/
JCB/Eurocard/Diners/Switch/Delta/
Eurocheque
🖵📞🍴♨🛁🐾

Swallow Hotel

Old Shire Lane, Waltham Abbey,
Essex EN9 3LX
Tel: (01992) 717170
Fax: (01992) 711841
⊖ **LOUGHTON**
Innovatively designed, new property,
off junction 26 of the M25. Two

restaurants, cocktail bar, residents'
lounge, leisure club and 163
bedrooms.
Bedrooms: 83 single, 27 double,
39 twin, 14 triple
Bathrooms: 163 en suite
Bed & Breakfast: single £130.00-
£140.00, double £150.00-160.00
Evening meal: 1800 (l.o. 2245)
Parking for: 260
Methods of payment: Mastercard/
Visa/Barclaycard/American Express/
JCB/Eurocard/Diners/Switch/Delta/
Eurocheque
🖵🌣📞🏌🗂🛏🍴♨🛁🐾

Thistle Brands Hatch Hotel

Brands Hatch, Dartford, Kent DA3 8PE
Tel: (01474) 854900
Fax: (01474) 853220
E-mail: brands.hatch@thistle.co.uk
⇌ **SWANLEY**
Set at the entrance to the world-
famous Grand Prix circuit. It is
situated close to the M20, M25 and
M26 and is easily accessible.
Bedrooms: 70 double, 51 twin
Bathrooms: 121 en suite
Bed only: single £59.00-£117.00,
double £59.00-£117.00
Evening meal: 1900 (l.o. 2130)
Parking for: 180
Methods of payment: Mastercard/
Visa/Barclaycard/American Express/
JCB/Eurocard/Diners/Switch/Delta/
Eurocheque
🖵🌣📞🏌🗂🛏🍴♨🛁🐾

Thistle Gatwick

Brighton Road, Horley, Surrey
RH6 8PH
Tel: (01293) 786992
Fax: (01293) 820625
E-mail: gatwick@thistle.co.uk
⇌ **HORLEY**
Modern hotel with some parts of
building dating back to early 16th
century. Courtesy coach to Gatwick
Airport, which is only two miles
away. Car parking available.
Bedrooms: 1 single, 33 double,
44 twin
Bathrooms: 78 en suite
Evening meal: 1900 (l.o. 2130)
Parking for: 185
Methods of payment: American
Express/Diners/Eurocheque
🖵🌣📞🏌🗂🛏🍴♨🐾

West Lodge Park

★ ★ ★ ★ Silver Award

Cockfosters Road, Hadley Wood,
Barnet, Hertfordshire EN4 0PY
Tel: (020) 8216 3900
Fax: (020) 8216 3937
E-mail: beales_westlodgepark@
compuserve.com
⊖ **COCKFOSTERS**
Georgian country house set in 35
acres of grounds in rolling countryside.
Bedrooms: 13 single, 33 double,
9 twin
Bathrooms: 55 en suite
Bed only: single £92.50, double
£130.00-£255.00
Evening meal: 1915 (l.o. 2130)
Parking for: 200
Methods of payment: Mastercard/
Visa/Barclaycard/American Express/
Diners/Switch/Delta/Eurocheque
🖵🌣📞🏌🗂🛏🍴♨🐾

APARTMENTS (SELF-CATERING)

130 Queensgate, London

130 Queens Gate, London SW7 5LE
Tel: (020) 7581 2322
Fax: (020) 7823 8488
E-mail: onethirty@compuserve.com
Situated in Kensington, each
apartment is self-contained with
modern, fully equipped kitchen,
luxury bathroom and maid service
six times weekly. Reception and
security available 24 hours.
Units: 54 serviced apartments
Prices: £875.50-£1,970.50 low
season, £875.50-£1,970.50 high
season
⚡🖵 LP 🛋🖥🍴

Acorn Management Service

Sutherland House, 70-78 West
Hendon Broadway, Edgware Road,
NW9 7BT
Tel: (020) 8202 3311
Fax: (020) 8202 6797
E-mail: info@acorn-london.co.uk
Self-contained, comfortably
furnished, fully equipped apartments
in central London near Bloomsbury,
West End and the Florida State
University London Study Centre in
Great Russell Street.
Units: 88 self-contained flats

Prices: £322.00-£867.00 low season, £392.00-£1,040.00 high season
⌐□ *LP* 🛋🖾 🍴

Apartment Services London

2 Sandwich Street, London
WC1H 9PL
Tel: (020) 7388 3558
Fax: (020) 7383 7255
E-mail: aptserltd.@aol.com
Self-contained, comfortably furnished, fully equipped apartments. Serviced weekly. Convenient for public transport, West End and theatres. Lets available from one week to a year.
Units: 100 self-contained flats, 1 house
Prices: £175.00-£1,500.00 low season, £175.00-£1,500.00 high season
⌐ *LP* 🛋🖾 🍴

Apartments West London incorporating Ealing Tourist Flats ★★—★★★ Self-Catering

94 Gordon Road, and 10 Hastings Road, London W13 8PT
Tel: (020) 8566 8187/
(01895) 233365
Fax: (020) 8566 7670
E-mail: info@apartmentswestlondon. com
Attractive apartments for the business or holiday traveller. Close to underground, restaurants and shopping arcades. Ideal location, with good parking.
Units: 3 self-contained studios, 3 self-contained flats
Prices: £295.00-£560.00 low season, £309.00-£590.00 high season
🚗⌐□ *LP* 🛋🖾 🍴

The Ascott Mayfair

49 Hill Street, Mayfair, London W1X 7FQ
Tel: (020) 7499 6868
Fax: (020) 7499 0705
E-mail: ascottmf@scotts.com.sg
A luxury, 56-apartment serviced residence in an art-deco style.
Units: 56 serviced apartments
🗆□⌐ *LP* 🛋🖾 🍴

Ashburn Garden Apartments

3 Ashburn Gardens, London SW7 4DG
Tel: (020) 7370 2663

Fax: (020) 7370 6743
E-mail: info@ashburngardens.co.uk
Well-established block of serviced apartments centrally located in Kensington. Attractively furnished with the accent on service and comfort.
Units: 24 serviced apartments
Prices: £560.00-£1,190.00 low season, £630.00-£1,295.00 high season
⌐□ *LP* 🛋🖾 🍴

Aston's Budget & Designer Studios

31 Rosary Gardens, South Kensington, London SW7 4NH
Tel: (020) 7590 6000
Fax: (020) 7590 6060
E-mail: sales@astons-apartments.com
Budget to luxury designer accommodation, with private bathrooms, air-conditioning, in restored Victorian townhouses in a centrally located, quiet, residential street. Very close to public transport, West End and theatres.
Units: 52 self-contained studios
Prices: £455.00-£1,155.00 low season, £455.00-£1,155.00 high season
⌐□ *LP* 🛋🖾 🍴

Athenaeum Hotel and Apartments

116 Piccadilly, London W1V 0BJ
Tel: (020) 7499 3464
Fax: (020) 7493 0644
E-mail: reservations@athenaeum hotel.com
Recent refurbishment of Apartments and Hotel to luxury standard. Guests have full use of services of adjoining Hotel, including luxury health spa.
Units: 33 serviced apartments
🗆⌐□ *LP* 🛋🖾 🍴

Beaufort House

45-47 Beaufort Gardens, Knightsbridge, London SW3 1PN
Tel: (020) 7584 2600
Fax: (020) 7584 6532
E-mail: info@beauforthouse.co.uk
Twenty one self-contained serviced apartments two minutes' walk from Harrods. Award Winner, London Tourism Award Self-Catering Holiday of the Year 1999.

Units: 21 serviced apartments
Prices: £1,439.38-£3,989.13 low season, £1,603.88-£4,482.63 high season
🗆⌐□ *LP* 🛋🖾 🍴

Beaumont Apartments

24 Combemartin Road, Southfields, London SW18 5PR
Tel: (020) 8789 2663/
07956 545431
Fax: (020) 8265 5499
E-mail: afriat@mistral.co.uk.
Well-appointed flats in leafy suburb within 30 minutes of the West End. Close to underground, Wimbledon tennis, A3 and M4. Easy access to M25, Gatwick and Heathrow. Ideal for business or holiday.
Units: 2 self-contained flats
Prices: £450.00-£490.00 low season, £500.00-£690.00 high season
🚗🗆⌐□ *LP* 🛋🖾 🍴

Belgard

PO Box 1026, London W2 1QE
Tel: (020) 7262 5273/
(01865) 514199
Fax: (01865) 512689
E-mail: nil.rey.apt@bigfoot.com
A Victorian terraced house near Marble Arch, containing self-contained one-bedroomed flats.
Units: 1 self-contained studio, 4 self-contained flats
Prices: £350.00-£400.00 low season, £475.00-£525.00 high season
🗆□ *LP* 🛋🖾 🍴

Bridge House
★★★★ Self-Catering

31 Falcon Way, Clippers Quay, London E14 9UP
Tel: (020) 7538 8980/
07973 857187
Fax: (020) 7538 8980
Two-bedroomed, luxury house. Spectacular waterside location in a tranquil oasis in the heart of Docklands. Private parking. Sunny waterside garden and master bedroom with balcony over the water.
Units: 1 house
Prices: £630.00 high season
🚗🗆⌐□ *LP* 🛋🖾 🍴

apartments

Carlton Court Residences Ltd

10 Down Street, London W1Y 7DS
Tel: (020) 7493 0597
Fax: (020) 7629 3225
E-mail: acu582dial.pipex.com
Carlton Court is a newly built exclusive block in the heart of Mayfair. Spacious apartments, fully serviced.
Units: 7 self-contained flats, 1 house
🚗 🗐 ↟ ⌷ *LP* 🖼 🖩

Citadines Barbican

7-21 Goswell Road, London EC1M 7AH
Tel: (020) 7766 3800
Fax: (020) 7766 3766
E-mail: orionuk@aol.com
A purpose-built apartotel located in the City of London and very near to the Barbican. All studios and apartments are well-equipped and furnished. Good value for money.
Units: 129 serviced apartments
Prices: £574.00–£651.00 low season, £574.00–£651.00 high season
🚗 🗐 ↟ *LP* 🖩

Citadines Holborn/ Covent Garden

94-99 High Holborn, London WC1V 6LF
Tel: (020) 7766 3800
Fax: (020) 7766 3866
Apartotel, comprising 192 studios and apartments over six floors. Modern furnishing. Opposite Holborn underground station.
Units: 152 self-contained studios, 40 self-contained flats
Prices: £637.00–£1,015.00 low season, £637.00–£1,015.00 high season
🚗 ⌷ *LP* 🖼

Clarendon House Apartments

48 Ranelagh Road, Ealing, London W5 5RJ
Tel: (01424) 212954/
(020) 8567 0314
Fax: (01424) 212954
E-mail: clarendon.house@lineone.net
A spacious apartment in a Victorian house or a purpose-built ground-floor apartment in a modern development. Both are in a pleasant

residential area with easy access to the underground and are close to shops and restaurants.
Units: 2 self-contained flats, 2 non self-contained flats
Prices: £300.00–£480.00 low season, £350.00–£550.00 high season
🚗 ↟ 🗐 ⌷ *LP* 🖼

Club Suites

4 Lower Sloane Street, and 11 and 19 Sloane Gardens, London SW1W 8BJ
Tel: (020) 7730 9131
Fax: (020) 7730 6146
E-mail: reservations@sloaneclub.co.uk
Two period properties just off Sloane Square. Some flats have two bathrooms and some have the use of private gardens.
Units: 16 self-contained flats
Prices: £1,028.00–£2,300.00 low season, £1,028.00–£2,300.00 high season
🗐 ↟ ⌷ *LP* 🖼 🖩 🍴

Craven Gardens Lodge

5-10 Craven Hill Gardens, London W2 3ES
Tel: (020) 7402 0393/
(020) 7402 0396
Fax: (020) 7262 7179
E-mail: lero@cravenlodge.swinternet.co.uk
Modern self-catering units, near shops, bus routes, the underground and Hyde Park.
Units: 50 self-contained studios, 50 self-contained flats
Prices: £350.00–£1,000.00 low season, £400.00–£1,350.00 high season
🗐 ⌷ *LP* 🖼 🖩 🍴

Crowne Plaza London – St James

41-54 Buckingham Gate, London SW1E 6AF
Tel: (020) 7834 6655/
(020) 7963 8384
Fax: (020) 7963 8385
E-mail: apartments@cplonsj.co.uk
Victorian-style apartments built in 1897 surrounding a central courtyard. Facilities include free health club, choice of three restaurants and cocktail bar.
Units: 83 self-contained flats

Prices: £1,717.00–£3,945.00 low season, £2,122.00–£4,870.00 high season
↟ ⌷ *LP* 🖼 🖩 🍴

Dolphin Square Hotel

Chichester Street, London SW1V 3LX
Tel: (020) 7798 8890
Fax: (020) 7798 8896
E-mail: reservations@dolphinsquarehotel.co.uk
Centrally located near Victoria and Westminster. Singles, doubles and one-, two- and three-bedroomed suites, combined with excellent facilities, such as two restaurants, bar, health and fitness spa which includes a swimming pool.
Units: 148 serviced apartments
Prices: £490.00–£2,520.00 low season, £490.00–£2,520.00 high season
🚗 ↟ ⌷ *LP* 🖼 🖩 🍴

Emperors Gate Short Stay Apartments

8 Knaresborough Place, Kensington, London SW5 0TG
Tel: (020) 7244 8409/
(020) 7373 0323
Fax: (020) 7373 6455
E-mail: info@apartment-hotels.com
Bringing the family? Emperors Gate can help. Family-owned and operated. Polly and Robert Arnold and their three children, understand your needs.
Units: 18 self-contained flats
Prices: £693.00–£1,113.00 low season, £693.00–£1,113.00 high season
🗐 ↟ ⌷ *LP* 🖼 🖩 🍴

Glenthurston Holiday Apartments

27-29 Canadian Avenue, London SE6 3AU
Tel: (020) 8690 3992
Fax: (020) 8265 5872
Large Victorian house converted into six flats with use of an indoor pool, sauna and steam room. Well located for central London. Homely relaxing atmosphere. Large garden and games room. Off-street parking.
Units: 6 self-contained flats
Prices: £340.00–£560.00 low season, £380.00–£625.00 high season
🚗 🗐 ⌷ *LP* 🖼 🖩 🍴

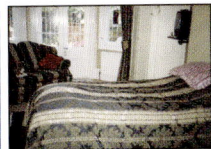

apartments

Grundy, Lytton & Partners

2 Violet Hill, St John's Wood, London
NW8 9EB
Tel: (020) 7624 1165/
07956 943772
Fax: (020) 7625 4552
Agent and operator for self-catering
accommodation in London.
Units: 2 self-contained studios,
20 self-contained flats, 4 houses,
5 serviced apartments
🖾🖵 *LP* 🖃🕮 🛠

Hamlet UK Ltd

★★–★★★ Self-Catering

4 Wellfield Avenue, London N10 2EA
Tel: (020) 8883 0024
Fax: (020) 8444 1118
E-mail: hamlet_uk@globalnet.co.uk/
~hamlet_uk
Friendly and personal service. Very
attractive surroundings. Comfortable
and clean accommodation close to
public transport and supermarket.
Units: 6 self-contained flats
Prices: £500.00–£675.00 low season,
£555.00–£725.00 high season
🚗🖾♦🖵 *LP* 🖃🕮 🛠

Kensington Guest House

72 Holland Park Avenue, London
W11 3QZ
Tel: (020) 7229 9233
Fax: (020) 7221 1077
E-mail: hotelondon@aol.com
Family-run guesthouse close to
public transport, with easy access to
Heathrow Airport. Full English
breakfast served in room. All rooms
have their own cooking facilities.
Units: 1 self-contained studio, 5 non
self-contained studios
🖾♦🖵 *LP* 🖃🛠

The Lexham

32-38 Lexham Gardens, London
W8 5JE
Tel: (020) 7559 4444
Fax: (020) 7559 4400
E-mail: reservations@lexham.com
Units: 31 serviced apartments
🚗🖾♦🖵 *LP* 🖃

London Country Apartments
Ltd
★★★★ Self-Catering and
Serviced Apartments

121 Cherry Orchard Road, East
Croydon, Croydon CR0 6BE

Tel: (020) 8686 8068/
07961 300017
Fax: (020) 8686 0678
E-mail: 101327.1320@compuserve.
com
Superbly furnished, purpose-built
apartments close to London. Ideal
for families and tourists, or business
relocations. Available all year. An
excellent hotel alternative.
Units: 1 self-contained studio,
17 serviced apartments
🚗🖾♦🖵 *LP* 🖃🕮 🛠

Moss Cottage

★★★★ Self-Catering

2 Moss Lane, Pinner, Middlesex
HA5 3AX
Tel: (020) 8868 5507
Fax: (020) 8868 5507
E-mail: bemail2@aol.com
Wing of 17th-century Grade II Listed
building.
Units: 1 cottage
Prices: £750.00–£750.00 low season,
£750.00–£800.00 high season
🖾🖵 *LP* 🖃🕮 🛠

NGH Apartments Ltd

Nell Gwynn House, Sloane Avenue,
London SW3 3AX
Tel: (020) 7589 1105
Fax: (020) 7589 9433
E-mail: reservations@nghapartments.
co.uk
Situated in the heart of Chelsea,
NGH offers 150 fully equipped and
serviced studios, one- and two-
bedroomed apartments. Close to
Sloane Square and South
Kensington underground. Many
sights within easy reach.
Units: 150 serviced apartments
Prices: £440.00–£1,320.00 low
season, £440.00–£1,320.00 high
season
🚗🖾♦🖵 *LP* 🖃🕮 🛠

Oakfield Estates

107 South Eden Park Road,
Beckenham, Kent BR3 3AX
Tel: (020) 8658 4441
Fax: (020) 8658 9198
E-mail: hols@oakfield.co.uk
Victorian mansion with a large
garden in a rural setting. Twenty five
minutes by rail to central London,
eight miles by road.
Units: 7 self-contained flats, 2 non
self-contained flats

Prices: £210.00–£600.00 low season,
£220.00–£650.00 high season
🚗🖾♦🖵 *LP* 🖃🕮 🛠

Orion Trafalgar Square

18-21 Northumberland Avenue,
London WC2N 5BJ
Tel: (020) 7766 3800/
(020) 7766 3700
Fax: (020) 7766 3866
E-mail: orionuk@aol.com
Orion's latest apartotel, right in the
heart of London, equipped to the
latest standards for one day, one
week, or more.
Units: 126 self-contained studios,
61 self-contained flats
Prices: £749.00–£1,400.00 low
season, £749.00–£1,400.00 high
season
🚗🖵 *LP* 🖃🕮

Park Lane Apartments

119-121 Park Lane, Mayfair, London
W1Y 3AE
Tel: (020) 7629 0763
Fax: (020) 7493 1308
E-mail: parklane@cpd.co.uk
Situated in an historically Listed
building, Park Lane Apartments are
in the heart of Mayfair.
Units: 101 self-contained flats
Prices: £700.00–£3,310.00 low
season, £777.00–£5,540.00 high
season
🖾♦🖵 *LP* 🖃🕮 🛠

Presidential Apartments

102 George Street, London W1U 5NT
Tel: (020) 7486 0097
Fax: (020) 7487 3624
E-mail: presapartmentslondon@
msn.com
Modern block with exclusive entrance
and lift. Estate office on second floor.
Units: 20 self-contained studios,
12 self-contained flats
Prices: £470.00–£655.00 low season,
£565.00–£865.00 high season
♦🖵 *LP* 🖃🕮 🛠

Presidential House

Presidential House, 1 University
Street, London WC1E 6JQ
Tel: (020) 7486 0097
Fax: (020) 7487 3624
E-mail: presapartmentslondon@
msn.com
Modern block with exclusive
entrance and lift to multi-bedroom,

home stay agencies

duplex apartments on the fifth and sixth floors.
Units: 12 self-contained flats
Prices: £365.00–£880.00 low season, £470.00–£1,150.00 high season
♦ ☐ LP 🖌 🖳 🍴

Royal Court Apartments

★–★★★ Self-Catering and Serviced Apartments

51-53 Gloucester Terrace, London W2 3DQ
Tel: (020) 7402 5077/ 0800 318798
Fax: (020) 7724 0286
E-mail: royalcourt@dial.pipex.com
Studios and apartments with kitchenette, dining area, satellite television and telephone. Located in central London, close to Paddington station and Lancaster Gate. Daily rates available.
Units: 28 self-contained studios, 43 serviced apartments
Prices: £65.00–£200.00 low season, £65.00–£257.00 high season
♦ ☐ LP 🖌 🖳 🍴

Scala House

21 Tottenham Street, London W1P 9PD
Tel: (020) 7580 6644
Fax: (020) 7636 3405
E-mail: ken@scala-house.co.uk
Family-run, comfortable apartments, in the heart of London. Goodge Street underground two minutes; British Museum six minutes.
Units: 34 self-contained flats, 34 serviced apartments
Prices: £665.00–£805.00 low season, £770.00–£910.00 high season
🖾 ♦ ☐ LP 🖌 🖳 🍴

Snow White Properties Ltd

55 Ennismore Gardens, Knightsbridge, London SW7 1AJ
Tel: (020) 7584 3307
Fax: (020) 7581 4686
E-mail: snow.white@virgin.net
Close to Harrods, Hyde Park, South Kensington museums and public transport. Friendly atmosphere. Located in a garden square.
Units: 13 self-contained flats
Prices: £680.00–£980.00 low season, £750.00–£1,020.00 high season
🖾 ♦ ☐ LP 🖌 🖳 🍴

Vancouver Studios

30 Princes Square, Bayswater, London W2 4NJ
Tel: (020) 7243 1270
Fax: (020) 7221 8678
E-mail: vancouverstudios@vienna-group.co.uk
Quality, serviced studios at reasonable rates, combining the convenience of a hotel with the privacy of an apartment. From one night.
Units: 45 self-contained studios
Prices: £400.00–£895.00 low season
♦ ☐ LP 🖳 🍴

The Village Property Services ★

98 Dollis Hill Avenue, London NW2 6QX
Tel: (020) 8452 5327
Fax: (020) 8452 0903
Within easy reach of the West End and the City. Convenient for theatres, museums, shopping, parks and London Zoo.
Units: 1 self-contained flat
Prices: £300.00–£700.00 low season, £350.00–£1,000.00 high season
🛋 🖩 ☐ LP 🖌 🖳 🍴

HOME STAY AGENCIES

Always Welcome Homes

11 Westerdale Road, London SE10 0LW
Tel: (020) 8858 0821
Fax: (020) 8858 7743
E-mail: bb@alwayswelcome.com
Contact: Marie Claire Trespeuch
Business hours: 0900-1900 hours
Minimum daily rate for single room: £21.00
Minimum daily rate for double/twin room: £35.00
Minimum weekly rate: £100.00 per person
Minimum length of stay: two nights
Established since 1982, Always Welcome Homes provides accommodation for school groups and students. Also over 100 well-selected private homes offering bed and breakfast in and outside London. French spoken.
Deposit: 30%

Cancellation policy: by arrangement
Areas covered: London and UK

At Home in London

70 Black Lion Lane, London W6 9BE
Tel: (020) 8748 1943
Fax: (020) 8748 2701
E-mail: info@athomeinlondon.co.uk
Contact: Maggie Dobson
Business hours: 0930-1730 hours
Minimum daily rate for single room: £30.00
Minimum daily rate for double/twin room: £52.00
Minimum weekly rate: £100.00 per person
Minimum length of stay: two consecutive nights
Bed and breakfast in over 90 homes in central locations, Knightsbridge, Mayfair, Kensington and West London. Carefully chosen homes, close to underground stations. Established in 1986.
Deposit: varies according to length of stay
Cancellation policy: if cancellation is made two weeks before arrival a new reservation for another date can be made. Deposit/reservation fee is not refundable
Areas covered: central London, zones 1 and 2

Best Bed & Breakfast in London

PO Box 2070, London W12 8QW
Tel: (020) 8742 9123 (24 hours)
Fax: (020) 8749 7084
E-mail: bestbandb@atlas.co.uk
Specialising in central London. Upmarket private homes.
Areas covered: inner and Greater London

Capital Accommodation

PO Box 57, Isleworth, Middlesex TW7 7JX
Tel: (020) 8560 5045 (answerphone)
Fax: (020) 8847 5835 (24 hours)
E-mail: carole@capital.fsnet.co.uk
Contact: Carole Pielichaty
Business hours: 0930-1800 hours
Minimum daily rate for single room: £23.00
Minimum daily rate for double/twin room: £44.00
Minimum length of stay: two nights

uality bed and breakfast in family
omes around London. Full English
reakfast, comfortable bedrooms,
hared or private bathrooms.
onvenient locations near stations.
eposit: 25%
ancellation policy: 100% within
8 hours of arrival
reas covered: West, South West
nd South East London

urostay

1 Eaton Road, Sidcup, Kent
A14 4PE
el: (020) 8309 5605
ax: (020) 8300 9690
ffers linguistic stays in family
ccommodation for students and
dults. Situated in the residential
reas of Eltham (London), Sidcup
nd Orpington (Kent). Twenty
inutes to central London and ten
inutes to the Millennium Dome.

appy Homes

eaufort Street, London SW3 5AD
el: (020) 7352 5121
ax: (020) 7352 5121
-mail: enquiries@happy-homes.com
ontact: Mrs Reynolds
usiness hours: 0930-1700 hours
Minimum daily rate for single room
ed and breakfast: £22.00
Minimum daily rate for double/twin
oom bed and breakfast: £36.00
Minimum weekly rate bed and
reakfast: £105.00 per person
Minimum length of stay: three
ights
appy Homes specialises in placing
isitors from all over the world into
rivate homes in central and South
Vest London.
eposit: by arrangement
ancellation policy: by arrangement
reas covered: central and South
Vest London

oliday Hosts

9 Cromwell Road, London
W19 8LF
el: (020) 8540 7942
ax: (020) 8540 2827
-mail: holiday.hosts@btinternet.com
usiness hours: 0900-1800 hours
Minimum daily rate for single
oom: £17.00
Minimum daily rate for a
ouble/twin room: £30.00

Minimum weekly rate bed and
breakfast: £98.00 per person (long-
term, students)
Specialists in comfortable, good-
quality accommodation in friendly
private homes in South and West
London. Near public transport and
with easy access to tourist
attractions. From £14.50–£35.00 per
person per night.
Deposit: £12.00 per person, £15.00
per person over three nights
Cancellation policy: two weeks
prior to arrival, refund less £5.00 per
person for admin charge
Areas covered: South and West
London

Homes Away

Doolittle Cottage, 38 Oakdale Road,
London E18 1JX
Tel: (020) 8530 2271
Fax: (020) 8530 2271
E-mail: homesaway@hotmail.com
Contact: Liz Garner
Business hours: 0900-1800 hours
Minimum daily rate for single
room: £20.00
Minimum daily rate for double/twin
room: £37.00
Minimum weekly rate: £115.00 per
person
Minimum length of stay: two nights
Select bed and breakfast, half-board
accommodation. Clean, friendly
homes close to underground
stations for central London. Groups
and vegetarians welcome. Credit
cards accepted.
Deposit: 10%
Areas covered: central London, City
Airport, North East London and
Essex

Host and Guest Service Ltd

103 Dawes Road, London SW6 7DU
Tel: (020) 7385 9922 (24 hours,
answerphone)/(020) 7385 3434
Fax: (020) 7386 7575
E-mail: acc@host-guest.co.uk
Contact: Carole Rutter
Business hours: 0900-1730 hours
Minimum daily rate for single
room: £16.50
Minimum daily rate for double/twin
room: £32.00
Minimum weekly rate: £80.00 per
person
Minimum length of stay: two nights

High-quality, good-value bed and
breakfast and student
accommodation for long and short
stays. Families catered for.
Deposit: 10%
Cancellation policy: up to eight
days before arrival 75% refunded,
between two and eight days 50%
refunded, less than two days no
refund, extreme circumstances
considered
Areas covered: all areas of Greater
London

The London Bed & Breakfast Agency Ltd

71 Fellows Road, London NW3 3JY
Tel: (020) 7586 2768
Fax: (020) 7586 6567
E-mail: stay@londonbb.com
Business hours: 0900-1800 hours
(Monday-Friday), 0900-1300
(Saturday)
Minimum daily rate for single room
bed and breakfast: £22.00
Minimum daily rate for double/twin
room bed and breakfast: £20.00
Minimum weekly rate for double
room bed and breakfast: £140.00
per person
Minimum length of stay: two nights
Quality accommodation in private
homes in and around the tourist
centres of London at prices to suit
all budgets.
Deposit: full payment required in
advance
Areas covered: North, South, South
West, West and central London

London First Choice Bed & Breakfast

111 Hill Rise, Greenford, Middlesex
UB6 8PE
Tel: (020) 8575 0559
Fax: (020) 8933 5778
E-mail: reserve@Lfca.co.uk
Contact: Reservations
Business hours: 0800-1900 hours
(Monday-Friday), 1000-1400 hours
(Saturday)
Minimum daily rate for single
room: £30.00–£70.00
Minimum daily rate for double/twin
room: £50.00–£90.00
Minimum length of stay: three
nights
Bed and breakfast with families in
private homes and small hotels in

home stay agencies

central London and London suburbs. Shared or private bath/shower, TV, tea and coffee making facilities.
Deposit: 20%
Cancellation policy: deposits are non-refundable. For hotel rooms cancelled within 48 hours the cost of one night's stay is due, for homes cancelled within seven days full balance is due
Areas covered: central and Greater London

London Holiday Accommodation

16 Chalk Farm Road, London NW1 8AJ
Tel: (020) 7485 0117
E-mail: sales@londonholiday.co.uk
Contact: Karen Walker
Business hours: 1200-1930 hours
Minimum daily rate: £30.00
Minimum weekly rate: £130.00 per person
Self-catering apartments and hosted homes all based in central London at incredibly reasonable prices. Airport pick-up available.
Deposit: £70.00-£200.00 per week depending on accommodation
Cancellation policy: 28 days before arrival and deposit will be refunded
Areas covered: Soho, Islington, Camden and Old Street

London Homestead Services

3 Coombe Wood Road, Kingston upon Thames, Surrey KT2 7JY
Tel: (020) 8949 4455 (24 hours)/ (020) 8541 0044
Fax: (020) 8549 5492
E-mail: lhs@netcomuk.co.uk
Business hours: 0900-2100 hours, daily
Minimum daily rate for single room: £15.00
Minimum daily rate for double/twin room: £18.00
Minimum weekly rate: £125.00 per person
Minimum length of stay: three days
Accommodation in zone 1 from £30.00 per person per night, zone 2 £20.00 per person per night and zone 3 £16.00 per person per night, bed and breakfast.
Deposit: 20%

Cancellation policy: deposit is non-returnable
Areas covered: all of London

Open Doors

1 Balcaskie Road, London SE9 1HQ
Tel: (020) 8480 9994
Fax: (020) 8480 9994
E-mail: patricia@opendoors.free serve.co.uk
Contact: Patricia or Kathy
Business hours: 0900-1700 hours
Minimum daily rate for single room bed and breakfast: £20.00
Minimum daily rate for double/twin room bed and breakfast: £20.00
Minimum weekly rate bed and breakfast: £140.00
Minimum length of stay: one night
Open Doors specialises in home stay accommodation for foreign students, tourists, large or small groups, in and around the South East area.
Deposit: 25%
Cancellation policy: loss of deposit or 10% of full amount if cancelled three days prior to arrival
Areas covered: South East London

Uptown Reservations

41 Paradise Walk, London SW3 4JL
Tel: (020) 7351 3445 (answerphone)
Fax: (020) 7351 9383
E-mail: inquiries@uptown.co.uk
Contact: Monica Barrington
Daily rate for single room: £70.00
Daily rate for double/twin room: £90.00
Minimum length of stay: one night
Providing upmarket accommodation in private host homes in the fashionable areas of central London. Every room has a private bathroom. Full continental breakfast provided.
Deposit: £20.00 minimum
Cancellation policy: deposit is non-refundable but may be applied to a later reservation if cancelled with seven days' notice
Areas covered: central London, primarily Kensington, Chelsea, Knightsbridge and Belgravia

Welcome Assured Ltd

1 Hillcrest Avenue, Edgware, Middlesex HA8 8NZ
Tel: (020) 8958 3996

Fax: (020) 8905 4747
Contact: Mrs Nicole Duke
Business hours: 0800-2200 hours (Sunday-Friday)
Minimum daily rate for single room bed and breakfast: £24.00
Minimum daily rate for double/twin room bed and breakfast: £45.00
Minimum weekly rate bed and breakfast: £165.00 per person
Home stay accommodation in selected host families for individuals and groups. A programme of activities, transport and escorts can be arranged.
Deposit: £100.00
Areas covered: North West London and suburbs

Welcome Homes & Hotels

21 Kellerton Road, London SE13 5R
Tel: (020) 8265 1212
Fax: (020) 8852 3243
E-mail: info@welcomehomes.co.uk
Contact: Pamela Burke
Business hours: 0900-1830
Minimum daily rate for single room bed and breakfast: £16.00
Minimum daily rate for double/twin room bed and breakfast: £14.00 per person
Minimum length of stay: three nights in B&B private homes, one night for hotels
Stay in friendly and affordable private bed and breakfast accommodation and small hotels in London and throughout the UK from only £14.00 per person per night bed and breakfast. Family rooms available. Organised tours of London and Britain also available. All major credit cards accepted.
Areas covered: central and Greater London

Worldwide Bed & Breakfast Association

PO Box 2070, London W12 8QW
Tel: (020) 8742 9123
Fax: (020) 8749 7084
E-mail: bestbandb@atlas.co.uk
Specialising in central London. Upmarket private homes.
Areas covered: inner and Greater London

GROUP AND YOUTH

SW1
Victoria/Westminster

Astor's Victoria Hotel

71 Belgrave Road, London SW1V 2BG
Tel: (020) 7834 3077
Fax: (020) 7932 0693
E-mail: astorhostels@msn.com
⊖/⇌ VICTORIA, ⊖ PIMLICO
Contact: Astor Hostels, 2-6 Inverness
Terrace, London W2 3HY
Contact Tel: (020) 7229 7866
Contact Fax: (020) 7229 1283
Budget accommodation within
walking distance of Victoria station,
Tate Gallery, Houses of Parliament,
Westminster Abbey and the Thames.
Caters for: Males, Females,
Individuals, Groups
Bedrooms: 1 double/twin
Total no of bedspaces: 60
Bathrooms: 5 public showers
Bed & Breakfast: single £14.00-
£20.00, double £29.00-£40.00
Open all year
Open over Christmas
⌁▥⊟☎🅿♦

Holland

63 Eccleston Square, London
SW1V 1PG
Tel: (020) 7834 9104
⊖/⇌ VICTORIA
Contact: Mr T Perkins, Head of
Personnel and Residential Services,
The London Hostels Association,
54 Eccleston Square, London
SW1V 1PG
Contact Tel: (020) 7828 3263
Contact Fax: (020) 7834 7146
Contact E-mail: bookings@london
hostels.co.uk
Budget accommodation in Victoria.
Three-course evening meal included.
Caters for: Males, Females,
Individuals, Groups
Bedrooms: 9 single, 13 double/twin
Total no of bedspaces: 84
Bathrooms: 12 public showers
Bed & Breakfast: single £18.50-
£22.50, double £37.00-£45.00
Open all year
Open over Christmas
⌁▥⊟☎🅿

University of Westminster

Wigram House, 84-99 Ashley
Gardens, Thirleby Road, London
SW1P 1HG
Tel: (020) 7911 5799/
(020) 7911 5796
Fax: (020) 7911 5141
E-mail: comserv@westminster.ac.uk
⊖/⇌ VICTORIA
Contact: Ms N Chanson, University
of Westminster Commercial
Services, Luxborough Suite, 35
Marylebone Road, London NW1 5LS
Refurbished seven-storey mansion
block in late-Victorian style, a few
minutes' walk from Victoria station,
offering single and twin rooms on a
self-catering basis.
Caters for: Males, Females,
Individuals, Groups
Bedrooms: 138 single, 28 double/twin
Total no of bedspaces: 194
Bathrooms: 55 public showers
Bed only: single £25.00-£35.00,
double £50.00-£70.00
Months open: June/July/August/
September
▯▥⊟☎🅿♿

Wellington Hall

King's College London, 71 Vincent
Square, London SW1P 2PA
Tel: (020) 7834 4740
Fax: (020) 7233 7709
E-mail: vac.bureau@kcl.ac.uk
**⊖/⇌ VICTORIA, ⊖ ST JAMES'S
PARK**
Contact: King's Campus Vacation
Bureau, 127 Stamford Street,
Waterloo, London SE1 9NQ
Contact Tel: (020) 7928 3777
Contact Fax: (020) 7928 5777
Wellington Hall is delightfully situated
in a quiet, green, central London
square and combines modern
facilities with traditional style. King's
College has seven additional halls of
residence throughout central London.
Caters for: Males, Females,
Individuals, Groups
Bedrooms: 39 single, 43 double/twin
Total no of bedspaces: 125
Bathrooms: 17 public showers
Bed & Breakfast: single £27.00,
double £42.00
Months open: January/April/June/
July/August/September
♿▯▥⊟☎🅿

W1
West End/Mayfair/Oxford Street

Carr-Saunders Hall

18-24 Fitzroy Street, London W1P 5AE
Tel: (020) 7323 9712
Fax: (020) 7580 4718
E-mail: saunders@lse.ac.uk
⊖ WARREN STREET
Contact: Mr A Fetnaci
Central for the West End, including
theatres, museums, parks, art
galleries and shopping in Oxford
Street and Covent Garden.
Caters for: Males, Females,
Individuals, Groups
Bedrooms: 132 single, 12 double/twin
Total no of bedspaces: 156
Bathrooms: 2 en suite, 35 public
showers
Bed & Breakfast: single £23.00,
double £38.00
Months open: March/April/July/
August/September
Parking for: 3
♿🚗▯▥⊟☎🅿♦

Oxford Street YHA

14-18 Noel Street, London W1V 3PD
Tel: (020) 7734 1618
Fax: (020) 7734 1657
⊖ OXFORD STREET
Contact: Ms D Bader
In the heart of Soho and near Oxford
Street, this hostel is a good sightseeing
base for individual travellers.
Sleeping accommodation is in small
bedrooms with individual security
lockers.
Minimum age: 6
Caters for: Males, Females, Individuals
Bedrooms: 24 double/twin, 5 triple,
3 family
Total no of bedspaces: 75
Bathrooms: 11 public showers
Open all year
Open over Christmas
♿▯▥⊟☎🅿♿

WC1
Bloomsbury/Strand/ Leicester Square

Ashlee House

261-265 Gray's Inn Road, London
WC1X 8QT

Caters for: Males, Females, Individuals, Groups
Bedrooms: 3 single, 4 double/twin, 1 triple, 1 family
Total no of bedspaces: 18
Bathrooms: 4 en suite, 6 public showers
Open all year
Open over Christmas
♿ 🚪 🖥 🛏 ☎ 🅿

Curzon House Hotel

58 Courtfield Gardens, London SW5 0NF
Tel: (020) 7581 2116
Fax: (020) 7835 1319
E-mail: info@curzonhousehotel.co.uk
⊖ **GLOUCESTER ROAD**
Contact: Mr C A Otter
Curzon House Hotel offers budget accommodation; guests have free use of the kitchen and dining room. Reduced weekly rates available from October to June.
Caters for: Males, Females, Individuals, Groups
Bedrooms: 2 single, 4 double/twin, 2 triple
Total no of bedspaces: 62
Bathrooms: 1 en suite, 5 public showers
Bed & Breakfast: single £15.00-£35.00, double £38.00-£48.00
Open all year
Open over Christmas
♿ 🚪 🛏 ☎ 🅿

Earl's Court YHA

38 Bolton Gardens, London SW5 0AQ
Tel: (020) 7373 7083
Fax: (020) 7835 2034
E-mail: earlscourt@yha.org.uk
⊖ **EARL'S COURT**
Contact: Mr D Green
Victorian townhouse in a residential area, close to shops, restaurants, nightlife and major tourist attractions. Comfortable dormitory accommodation.
Minimum age: 5
Caters for: Males, Females, Individuals
Bedrooms: 2 triple, 4 family
Total no of bedspaces: 155
Bathrooms: 22 public showers

Bed & Breakfast: single £18.67-£20.75
Open all year
Open over Christmas
♿ 🚪 🖥 🛏 ☎ 🅿 ⛲

Halpin

97 Queen's Gate, London SW7 5AB
Tel: (020) 7373 4180
Fax: (020) 7370 7606
⊖ **SOUTH KENSINGTON**
Contact: Mr T Perkins, Head of Personnel and Residential Services, The London Hostels Association, 54 Eccleston Square, London SW1V 1PG
Contact Tel: (020) 7828 3263
Contact Fax: (020) 7834 7146
Contact E-mail: bookings@london hostels.co.uk
Self-catering accommodation situated in South Kensington and convenient for museums.
Caters for: Males, Females, Individuals
Bedrooms: 23 single, 68 double/twin
Total no of bedspaces: 145
Bathrooms: 14 public showers
Bed only: single £15.50-£19.50, double £31.00-£39.00
Open all year
Open over Christmas
🚪 🖥 🛏 ☎ 🅿

Imperial College Reservations

Imperial College Conference Office, Watts Way, Prince's Gardens, London SW7 1LU
Tel: (020) 7594 9507/ (020) 7594 9511
Fax: (020) 7594 9504
E-mail: reservations@ic.ac.uk
⊖ **SOUTH KENSINGTON**
Contact: Mr P Hudson
Contact Tel: (020) 7594 9525/ (020) 7594 9494
University accommodation overlooking attractive gardens in South Kensington. Museums, Royal Albert Hall, Hyde Park and Harrods located nearby. Superior en suite student study-bedrooms are available next to Royal Albert Hall.
Minimum age: 10
Caters for: Males, Females, Individuals, Groups
Bedrooms: 852 single, 152 double/twin
Total no of bedspaces: 1,135
Bathrooms: 248 en suite, 165 public showers

Bed & Breakfast: single £35.00-£58.00, double £55.00-£85.00
Months open: March/April/July/August/September
Parking for: 300
♿ 🅿 🚪 🖥 🛏 ☎ 🅿 🔍

Regina

110 Gloucester Road, London SW7 4RJ
Tel: (020) 7373 5151
Fax: (020) 7370 7580
⊖ **GLOUCESTER ROAD**
Contact: Mr T Perkins, The London Hostels Association, 54 Eccleston Square, London SW1V 1PG
Contact Tel: (020) 7828 3263
Contact Fax: (020) 7834 7146
Contact E-mail: bookings@london hostels.co.uk
Single, double and dormitory rooms available. Prices for dormitory rooms include bed, breakfast and a three-course evening meal.
Caters for: Males, Females, Individuals, Groups
Bedrooms: 12 single, 26 double/twin
Total no of bedspaces: 105
Bathrooms: 10 public showers
Bed & Breakfast: single £18.50-£22.50, double £37.00-£45.00
Open all year
Open over Christmas
🚪 🖥 🛏 ☎ 🅿

EC1/4
City of London

City of London YHA

36 Carter Lane, London EC4V 5AB
Tel: (020) 7236 4965
Fax: (020) 7236 7681
E-mail: city@yha.org.uk
⊖ **ST PAUL'S,**
⊖/⇌ **BLACKFRIARS**
Contact: Mr S Collier
In the centre of the City of London in an area of winding narrow streets, this hostel is a former school for choirboys of St Paul's Cathedral. Please check prices at time of reservation.
Minimum age unaccompanied: 14
Caters for: Males, Females, Individuals, Groups
Bedrooms: 3 single, 7 double/twin, 7 triple, 10 family

group and youth

Total no of bedspaces: 193
Bathrooms: 2 en suite, 10 public showers
Bed & Breakfast: single £20.50-£27.50, double £41.00-£55.00
Open all year
Open over Christmas
🛏🖥📺🍴🚃🔌📞🅿🐾�&

Finsbury Residences City University

Bastwick Street, London EC1V 3PE
Tel: (020) 7477 8811
Fax: (020) 7477 8810
⊖ **ANGEL/OLD STREET**
Contact: Ms J Morgan
Finsbury Residences comprises two modern halls built in the mid-seventies. It is close to the Barbican Arts Centre and Upper Street.
Caters for: Males, Females, Individuals, Groups
Bedrooms: 320 single
Bathrooms: 52 public showers
Bed & Breakfast: single £19.00-£35.00, double £38.00-£50.00
Total no of bedspaces: 320
Methods of payment: Mastercard/Visa/Barclaycard/American Express/Eurocheque
🛏🖥📺🍴🚃🔌📞🅿

Rosebery Avenue Hall

90 Rosebery Avenue, London EC1R 4TY
Tel: (020) 7278 3251
Fax: (020) 7278 2068
E-mail: rosebery@lse.ac.uk
⊖ **ANGEL**
Contact: Ms M Zanfal
Modern hall of residence convenient for Oxford Street and the West End. Every room with washbasin. Lift. Television and meals available.
Minimum age unaccompanied: 15
Caters for: Males, Females, Individuals, Groups
Bedrooms: 157 single, 109 double/twin, 13 triple
Total no of bedspaces: 448
Bathrooms: 18 en suite, 70 public showers
Bed & Breakfast: single £26.00-£32.00, double £36.00-£46.00
Months open: March/April/July/August/September
🛏🖥📺🍴🚃🔌📞🅿⚒

W8/11 Kensington/Notting Hill/ Hammersmith/West Kensington

Bowden Court

24 Ladbroke Road, London W11 3NN
Tel: (020) 7727 5665
Fax: (020) 7229 2534
⊖ **NOTTING HILL GATE**
Contact: Mr T Perkins, Head of Personnel and Residential Services, The London Hostels Association, 54 Eccleston Square, London SW1V 1PG
Contact Tel: (020) 7828 3263
Contact Fax: (020) 7834 7146
Contact E-mail: bookings@london hostels.co.uk
Single, double and dormitory rooms available. Dormitory prices include bed, breakfast and a three-course evening meal.
Caters for: Males, Females, Individuals, Groups
Bedrooms: 62 single, 122 double/twin
Total no of bedspaces: 450
Bathrooms: 21 public showers
Bed & Breakfast: single £18.50-£22.50, double £37.00-£45.00
Open all year
Open over Christmas
🖥📺🍴🚃📞🅿

Holland House YHA

Holland Walk, Kensington, London W8 7QN
Tel: (020) 7937 0748
Fax: (020) 7376 0667
E-mail: hollandhouse@yha.org.uk
⊖ **HIGH STREET KENSINGTON**
Contact: Mr A Lamb
Modern hostel incorporating part of a Jacobean mansion, set in a park with woodland, lawns and playing field. Prices to be advised on application.
Minimum age: 5
Caters for: Males, Females, Individuals, Groups
Bedrooms: 1 single, 1 double/twin, 1 triple, 1 family
Total no of bedspaces: 201
Bathrooms: 38 public showers
Bed & Breakfast: single £18.50-£20.50
Open all year
Open over Christmas
🛏🖥📺🚃📞🅿

North West London

Belsize

40 Belsize Park Gardens, London NW3 4NA
Tel: (020) 7722 8131
Fax: (020) 7483 0889
⊖ **BELSIZE PARK**
Contact: Mr T Perkins, Head of Personnel and Residential Services, The London Hostels Association, 54 Eccleston Square, London SW1V 1PG
Contact Tel: (020) 7828 3263
Contact Fax: (020) 7834 7146
Contact E-mail: bookings@london hostels.co.uk
Hostel offering budget accommodation near Belsize Park station. Three-course evening meal included in the price.
Caters for: Males, Females, Individuals, Groups
Bedrooms: 19 single, 48 double/twin
Total no of bedspaces: 144
Bathrooms: 16 public showers
Bed & Breakfast: single £18.50-£22.50, double £37.00-£45.00
Open all year
Open over Christmas
🖥📺🚃📞🅿

Hampstead Heath YHA

4 Wellgarth Road, Golders Green, London NW11 7HR
Tel: (020) 8458 7196/(020) 8458 9054
Fax: (020) 8209 0546
E-mail: hampstead@yha.org.uk
⊖ **GOLDERS GREEN**
Contact: Ms B Robinson
Built in 1915, this three-storey building stands amongst beautiful landscaped gardens and is close to Hampstead Heath, Golders Green and public transport for central London.
Minimum age unaccompanied: 14
Caters for: Males, Females, Individuals, Groups
Bedrooms: 14 double/twin, 9 triple, 14 family
Total no of bedspaces: 199
Bathrooms: 22 public showers
Bed & Breakfast: single £20.50-£47.00, double £41.00-£47.00
Open all year
Open over Christmas
Parking for: 8
🛏🚗🖥📺🍴🚃🔌📞🅿🐾⚒

group and youth

King's College London Hampstead Campus

Kidderpore Avenue, London NW3 7ST
Tel: (020) 7435 3564
Fax: (020) 7431 4402
E-mail: vac.bureau@kcl.ac.uk
↤ FINCHLEY ROAD
Contact: King's Campus Vacation Bureau, 127 Stamford Street, Waterloo, London SE1 9NQ
Contact Tel: (020) 7928 3777
Contact Fax: (020) 7928 5777
University campus offering single and twin rooms in modern and turn-of-the-century buildings. Function rooms available.
Caters for: Males, Females, Individuals, Groups
Bedrooms: 252 single, 124 double/twin
Total no of bedspaces: 500
Bathrooms: 40 public showers
Bed only: single £18.00, double £31.00
Months open: June/July/August/September

Regents College

Inner Circle, Regent's Park, London NW1 4NS
Tel: (020) 7487 7495
Fax: (020) 7487 7602
E-mail: markhamt@regents.ac.uk
↤ BAKER STREET
Contact: Ms T Markham
International college and affiliated teaching organisations on central London campus, with one large hall of residence, Reid Hall. Groups only accommodation for advance bookings. Individuals can book one week maximum in advance.
Caters for: Males, Females, Groups
Bedrooms: 22 single, 78 double/twin, 16 triple
Total no of bedspaces: 226
Bathrooms: 5 en suite, 40 public showers
Bed only: single £26.00-£37.00, double £51.00-£53.00
Months open: January/May/June/July/August
Parking for: 45

St Pancras YHA

79-81 Euston Road, London NW1 2QS
Tel: (020) 7388 9998
Fax: (020) 7388 6766
E-mail: stpancras@yha.org.uk
↤/⇄ EUSTON/KING'S CROSS
Contact: Ms J Bancroft
New YHA hostel, near to stations. Ideal for staying in London. Short walk to Camden Market.
Minimum age unaccompanied: 14
Caters for: Males, Females, Individuals
Bedrooms: 11 double/twin, 13 family
Total no of bedspaces: 150
Bathrooms: 33 en suite, 14 public showers
Bed only: single £23.50-£28.00
Open all year
Open over Christmas

University of Westminster

Marylebone Road Hall of Residence, 35 Marylebone Road, London NW1 5LS
Tel: (020) 7911 5799/(020) 7911 5796
Fax: (020) 7911 5141
E-mail: comserv@westminster.ac.uk
↤ BAKER STREET
Contact: Ms N Chanson, University of Westminster Commercial Services, Luxborough Suite, 35 Marylebone Road, London NW1 5LS
Student residence in central London, offering single study-bedrooms on a self-catering basis or with meals. Rooms on the higher floors offer breathtaking views of London.
Caters for: Males, Females, Individuals, Groups
Bedrooms: 220 single
Total no of bedspaces: 220
Bathrooms: 84 public showers
Bed only: single £25.00-£35.00
Months open: June/July/August/September

North London

Kent House

325 Green Lanes, London N4 2ES
Tel: (020) 8802 0800/(020) 8802 5100
Fax: (020) 8802 9070
E-mail: kenthall@dircon.co.uk
↤ MANOR HOUSE
Special off-season and weekly rates. Groups and school parties welcome. Facilities for self-catering available. Ten minutes from central London.
Minimum age unaccompanied: 16
Caters for: Males, Females, Individuals, Groups
Bedrooms: 3 single, 13 double/twin
Total no of bedspaces: 34
Bathrooms: 6 public showers
Bed & Breakfast: single £25.00-£27.00, double £36.00-£38.00
Open all year
Open over Christmas
Parking for: 4

University of Westminster

Furnival House, Chomeley Park, Highgate, London N6 5EU
Tel: (020) 7911 5799/(020) 7911 5796
Fax: (020) 7911 5141
E-mail: comserv@wmin.ac.uk
↤ ARCHWAY
Contact: Ms N Chanson, University of Westminster Commercial Services, Luxborough Suite, 35 Marylebone Road, London NW1 5LS
Contact Tel: (020) 7911 5799/(020) 7911 5807
Contact E-mail: comserv@westminster.ac.uk
Refurbished Edwardian hall of residence in Highgate Village, situated in its own grounds, within walking distance of Waterlow Park and Hampstead Heath. Good quality accommodation in single rooms on a self-catering basis.
Minimum age: 12
Caters for: Males, Females, Individuals, Groups
Bedrooms: 113 single
Total no of bedspaces: 113
Bathrooms: 16 public showers
Bed only: single £25.00-£35.00
Months open: June/July/August/September
Parking for: 6

University of Westminster – Alexander Fleming Halls of Residence

3 Hoxton Market, London N1 6HG
Tel: (020) 7911 5799/(020) 7911 5796
Fax: (020) 7911 5141
E-mail: comserv@westminster.ac.uk
↤/⇄ OLD STREET

group and youth

Contact: Ms N Chanson, University of Westminster Commercial Services, Luxborough Suite, 35 Marylebone Road, London NW1 5LS
Situated on the edge of the City, the halls offer good quality single study-bedrooms in self-contained flats of four to eight. The halls are well served by public transport and are ideal for sightseeing.
Caters for: Males, Females, Individuals, Groups
Bedrooms: 186 single
Total no of bedspaces: 186
Bed only: single £25.00–£35.00
Months open: June/July/August/ September
Parking for: 5

Walter Sickert Hall City University

Graham Street, London N1 8LA
Tel: (020) 7477 8822
Fax: (020) 7477 8823
⊖ ANGEL
Contact: Mr I Gibbard
Contact E-mail: i.gibbard@city.ac.uk
Hall of residence with all en suite rooms, close to Angel underground station and Camden Market, with easy access to the West End.
Minimum age: 7
Caters for: Males, Females, Individuals, Groups
Bedrooms: 226 single, 8 double/twin
Total no of bedspaces: 242
Bathrooms: 234 en suite
Bed & Breakfast: single £30.00, double £50.00
Months open: July/August/ September
Parking for: 6

East London

Cordwainers Court

St Thomas Square, London E9 7PS
Tel: (020) 8985 6685/
(020) 8985 6781
Fax: (020) 8525 1756
E-mail: hor@cordwainers.ac.uk
⊖ BETHNAL GREEN
Contact: Ms K Gregory, Cordwainers College, 182 Mare Street, London E8 3RE

Cordwainers Court offers quality self-catering accommodation for students and educational personnel. Four-bedroomed flats overlooking pleasant gardens near the City. Minimum stay is three nights.
Caters for: Males, Females, Individuals, Groups
Bedrooms: 87 single
Total no of bedspaces: 87
Bathrooms: 23 public showers
Bed & Breakfast: single £15.00–£18.00
Months open: July/August
Parking for: 12

Queen Mary and Westfield College

Mile End Road, London E1 4NS
Tel: (020) 7882 3642/
(020) 7882 3103
Fax: (020) 8983 0146
E-mail: holiday@qmw.ac.uk
⊖ MILE END
Contact: Ms S Mussett
Contact E-mail: s.e.mussett@qmw.ac.uk
Modern canal-side city campus, with clean and simple student accommodation, available in the summer. Suitable for groups, conferences and self-catering.
Caters for: Males, Females, Individuals, Groups
Bedrooms: 561 single
Total no of bedspaces: 561
Bathrooms: 156 en suite, 91 public showers
Bed & Breakfast: single £31.40–£41.50, double £62.80–£83.00
Months open: June/July/August/ September

Sir John Cass Hall

150 Well Street, London E9 7LQ
Tel: (020) 8533 2529
Fax: (020) 8525 0633
E-mail: enquiries@sirjohncass. demon.co.uk
⊖ BETHNAL GREEN
Contact: Ms A Young, Claredale House, Claredale Street, Bethnal Green, London E2 6PE
Contact Tel: (020) 7739 7440
Contact Fax: (020) 7729 5570
Student halls offering comfortable accommodation during vacation

times. Close to the City. Reasonable rates for individuals and groups.
Minimum age unaccompanied: 16
Caters for: Males, Females, Individuals, Groups
Bedrooms: 131 single
Total no of bedspaces: 131
Bathrooms: 12 public showers
Bed & Breakfast: single £16.00–£20.00
Months open: July/August/ September
Parking for: 20

South East London

Bankside House

24 Sumner Street, London SE1 9JA
Tel: (020) 7633 9877
Fax: (020) 7574 6730
E-mail: bankside-reservation@lse.ac.uk
⊖ SOUTHWARK
Contact: Mr R Anderson
Situated on the South Bank next to the Globe Theatre. Bankside House provides modern, en suite bed and breakfast accommodation, with a restaurant, television, bar and good facilities.
Caters for: Males, Females, Individuals, Groups
Bedrooms: 290 single, 227 double/twin, 14 triple, 4 family
Total no of bedspaces: 833
Bathrooms: 308 en suite, 25 public showers
Bed & Breakfast: single £30.00–£60.00, double £55.50–£70.00
Months open: July/August/ September
Parking for: 30

Butlers Wharf Residence

11 Gainsford Street, London SE1 2NE
Tel: (020) 7407 7164
Fax: (020) 8403 0847
⊖/⇌ LONDON BRIDGE,
⊖ TOWER HILL
Contact: Mr G Kane
Modern building on the South Bank of the Thames. Surrounded by many historic buildings. There are many cafes and restaurants nearby.
Caters for: Males, Females, Individuals, Groups

Bedrooms: 250 single, 12 double/twin
Total no of bedspaces: 274
Bathrooms: 98 public showers
Months open: July/August/
September

The Dover Castle Hostel and Bar

6A Great Dover Street, London
SE1 4XW
Tel: (020) 7403 7773
Fax: (020) 7782 2059
E-mail: www.dovercastlehostel@hot
mail.com

**⊖/⇌ LONDON BRIDGE/
WATERLOO, ⊖ BOROUGH**
Contact: Ms S Stone
Bed/Breakfast accommodation.
Backpackers and travellers between
the ages of 18-40. Dormitory style
rooms.
Caters for: Males, Females,
Individuals, Groups
Bedrooms: 1 triple, 1 family,
3 dormitory
Total no of bedspaces: 65
Bathrooms: 6 public showers
Bed & Breakfast: single £14.00
Open all year

Great Dover Street Apartments

165 Great Dover Street, London
SE1 4XA
Tel: (020) 7407 0069
Fax: (020) 7378 7973
E-mail: vac.bureau@kcl.ac.uk
**⊖/⇌ LONDON BRIDGE,
⊖ BOROUGH**
Contact: King's Campus Vacation
Bureau, 127 Stamford Street,
London SE1 9NQ
Contact Tel: (020) 7928 3777
Contact Fax: (020) 7928 5777
A modern residence built around a
courtyard and located in a historic
area of London.
Caters for: Males, Females,
Individuals, Groups
Bedrooms: 700 single
Total no of bedspaces: 700
Bathrooms: 70 public showers
Bed only: single £31.00, double
£49.00
Months open: July/August/
September

Henry Wood House

10 Halsmere Road, Camberwell,
London SE5 9LN
Tel: (020) 7735 3158
Fax: (020) 7582 7466
⊖ OVAL
Contact: Mr D Crook
Hall of residence with study-
bedrooms and communal bath, WC
and kitchen facilities. The site is split
between two buildings.
Minimum age: 10
Caters for: Males, Females,
Individuals, Groups
Bedrooms: 25 single, 23 double/
twin, 5 triple
Total no of bedspaces: 86
Bathrooms: 14 public showers
Bed only: single £6.00-£10.00,
double £10.00-£17.00
Months open: July/August

King's College Hall

King's College London, Champion
Hill, London SE5 8AN
Tel: (020) 7733 2166
Fax: (020) 7737 0235
E-mail: vac.bureau@kcl.ac.uk
⇌ DENMARK HILL
Contact: King's Campus Vacation
Bureau, 127 Stamford Street,
London SE1 9NQ
Contact Tel: (020) 7928 3777
Contact Fax: (020) 7928 5777
Set in pleasant, quiet grounds this hall
offers budget accommodation. Three
miles from Westminster and the City.
Caters for: Males, Females, Groups
Bedrooms: 450 single
Total no of bedspaces: 450
Bathrooms: 70 public showers
Bed & Breakfast: single £19.50
Months open: June/July/August/
September
Parking for: 60

NBH 159 Great Dover Street

159 Great Dover Street, London
SE1 4WW
Tel: (020) 7403 1997
Fax: (020) 7403 2342
E-mail: nbha@159gds.ndo.co.uk
⊖ BOROUGH
Contact: Ms V Francese
Brand new residence close to major
attractions. All rooms are en suite

and have shared use of kitchens,
launderette and café-bar.
Caters for: Males, Females,
Individuals, Groups
Bedrooms: 285 single,
1 double/twin
Total no of bedspaces: 287
Bathrooms: 286 en suite, 1 public
shower
Bed & Breakfast: single £26.78-
£30.90
Months open: July/August/
September

Rotherhithe YHA and Conference Centre

Salter Road, London SE16 5PR
Tel: (020) 7232 2114
Fax: (020) 7237 2919
⊖ ROTHERHITHE
Contact: Mr R E Stackhouse
Purpose-built hostel offering modern
furnishings, central heating and
privacy. All bedrooms have en suite
facilities. Sleeping accommodation is
mainly in small bedrooms with
modern bunks and security lockers.
Caters for: Males, Females,
Individuals, Groups
Bedrooms: 22 double/twin, 16 family
Total no of bedspaces: 320
Bathrooms: 7 public showers
Open all year
Open over Christmas

St Christophers Inns

121 Borough High Street, London
Bridge, London SE1 1NP
Tel: (020) 7407 1856
Fax: (020) 7403 7715
E-mail: bookings@st-christophers.co.
uk
⊖/⇌ LONDON BRIDGE
Contact: Mr R Bradford
Three minutes' walk from London
Bridge or Borough underground
stations. Grade I Listed building with
an amazing history. Late-licensed
pub within the building, with a chill-
out room open 24 hours. Also a
coffee shop.
Caters for: Males, Females,
Individuals, Groups
Bedrooms: 2 double/twin, 9 family
Total no of bedspaces: 84

caravan and camping sites

Bathrooms: 13 public showers
Bed only: single £12.00–£17.50
Open all year
Open over Christmas
⌂ ▯ ▥ ◿ ☎ ▱ ◕

Stamford Street Apartments King's Campus Vacation Bureau

127 Stamford Street, Waterloo,
London SE1 9NQ
Tel: (020) 7873 2960/
(020) 7873 2962
Fax: (020) 7873 2964
E-mail: vac.bureau@kcl.ac.uk
⊖/⇌ WATERLOO
Contact Tel: (020) 7928 3777
Contact Fax: (020) 7928 5777
A modern residence with 556 single
bedrooms arranged in units of four
to nine rooms. All rooms are en
suite with shower.
Caters for: Males, Females,
Individuals, Groups
Bedrooms: 556 single
Bathrooms: 556 en suite
Bed only: single £34.00
Months open: July/August/
September
⌂ ▥ ☎ ▱ ⛽

University of Westminster

International House, 1-5 Lambeth
Road, London SE1 6HU
Tel: (020) 7911 5799/
(020) 7911 5796
Fax: (020) 7911 5141
E-mail: comserv@westminster.ac.uk
⊖/⇌ WATERLOO,
⊖ LAMBETH NORTH
Contact: Ms N Chanson, University
of Westminster Commercial
Services, Luxborough Suite,
35 Marylebone Road, London
NW1 5LS
Small hall of residence, 15 minutes
from the Houses of Parliament,
offering good quality
accommodation in single or twin
rooms on self-catering basis.
Minimum age: 12
Caters for: Males, Females,
Individuals, Groups
Bedrooms: 63 single, 9 double/twin
Total no of bedspaces: 81
Bathrooms: 18 public showers
Bed only: single £25.00–£35.00,
double £50.00–£70.00

Months open: June/July/August/
September
Parking for: 2
⌂ ▰ ▯ ▥ ◿ ☎ ▱

London's Country

Brunel University College

300 St Margaret's Road,
Twickenham, TW1 1PT
Tel: (020) 8891 0121
Fax: (020) 8891 8270
E-mail: pauline.grey@brunel.ac.uk
⊖/⇌ RICHMOND,
⇌ ST MARGARET'S
Contact: Mrs P Oprey
Contact Tel: (020) 8891 0121/
(020) 8891 8242
Contact Fax: (020) 8891 8348
This pleasant campus is on the
Thames near Richmond, within easy
reach of Heathrow and central
London.
Caters for: Males, Females, Groups
Bedrooms: 314 single, 15 double/twin
Total no of bedspaces: 344
Bathrooms: 60 public showers
Months open: April/July/August/
September
Parking for: 200
▰ ▯ ▥ ◿ ☎ ▱ ◕ ⛽

Brunel University Conference Centre

Conference Office, Brunel University,
Uxbridge, Middlesex UB8 3PH
Tel: (01895) 238353
Fax: (01895) 203142
E-mail: conference@brunel.ac.uk
⊖ UXBRIDGE
Contact: Mrs V Tomlinson
En suite and standard bedrooms,
cafeteria or silver service meals,
purpose-built theatres and
classrooms, audio and visual aids
and sports facilities all available.
Caters for: Males, Females,
Individuals, Groups
Bedrooms: 695 single, 3 double/twin
Total no of bedspaces: 698
Bathrooms: 464 en suite, 85 public
showers
Bed & Breakfast: single £35.00,
double £67.00
Months open: June/July/August/
September
Parking for: 2,000
▰ ▥ ◿ ☎ ▱ ◕ ⛽

CARAVAN AND CAMPING SITES

Crystal Palace Caravan Club Site
★★★★ Touring and Camping Park

Crystal Palace Parade, London
SE19 1UF
Tel: (020) 8778 7155
Fax: (020) 8676 0980
⇌ CRYSTAL PALACE
Contact: The Warden
Busy site on A212, off A205 South
Circular Road. Good transport links
to London.
Total no of pitches: 150
Daily prices: Prices on application
Open: All year

Lee Valley Campsite
★★★★ Camping Park

Sewardstone Road, Chingford E4 7RA
Tel: (020) 8529 5689
Fax: (020) 8559 4070
Contact: Mr D S Pegg
⇌ CHINGFORD,
⊖ WALTHAMSTOW CENTRAL
Spacious park with well-planned
facilities on the A112 between
Chingford and Waltham Abbey, 12
miles from central London. Wide
range of recreational activities in the
surrounding area of the Lee Valley
Park.
Total no of pitches: 200
Daily prices: Prices on application
Open: April-October
▰

Lee Valley Leisure Centre ★★★★ Touring Park

Meridian Way, London N9 0AS
Tel: (020) 8345 6666/
(020) 8803 6900
Fax: (020) 8884 4975
⇌ EDMONTON GREEN
Contact: Mr A Butler/Mr and
Mrs J Cartlidge
This site is part of Lee Valley Leisure
Centre with a wide range of sporting
and leisure activities. Fast train
service to central London within a
short bus ride, and the countryside
of Epping Forest and Lee Valley
nearby.
Total no of pitches: 160
Daily prices: £10.70 per pitch,
£2.85 electrical hook-up

caravan and camping sites

Open: All year except 25,26 December and 1 January
🚐

Lee Valley Park, Eastway Cycle Circuit

Quarter Mile Lane, Stratford, London E15 2EN
Tel: (020) 8534 6085
Fax: (020) 8536 0959
⊖ LEYTON
Contact: Ben Darter
Part of the 40-acre landscaped park which is the home of the unique

Eastway Cycle circuit, only four miles from the City of London. Well-maintained surroundings and a wide range of modern facilities.
Total no of pitches: 100
Daily prices: £5.35 per person, per night
Open: March-October
🚐

Tent City – Hackney

Millfields Road, Hackney, London E5 0AR
Tel: (020) 8985 7656

Fax: (020) 8749 9074
E-mail: tentcity@btinternet.com
⊖ LEYTON
Contact: Anna Stubbs
London's most central campsite and tented hostel. Canal-side site in nature reserve. Friendly and peaceful atmosphere. Run by international staff. Profits to charity.
Total no of pitches: 200
Daily prices: £5.00 per person
Open: July-August
🚐

Advertisers' Index

indexes

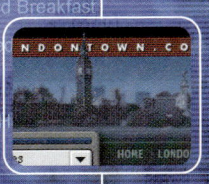

indexes